# The Tyndale Old Testament Commentaries

*General Editor:*
PROFESSOR D. J. WISEMAN, O.B.E., M.A., D.LIT., F.B.A., F.S.A.

## EZRA and NEHEMIAH

# EZRA
## and
# NEHEMIAH

*AN INTRODUCTION AND COMMENTARY*

by

THE REV. DEREK KIDNER, M.A., A.R.C.M.
*formerly Warden of Tyndale House, Cambridge*

INTER-VARSITY PRESS
LEICESTER, ENGLAND
DOWNERS GROVE, ILLINOIS, U.S.A.

**Inter-Varsity Press**
*38 De Montfort Street, Leicester LE1 7GP, England*
*Box 1400, Downers Grove, Illinois 60515 U.S.A.*

© *Derek Kidner 1979*

*Inter-Varsity Press, England, is the publishing division of the Universities and
Colleges Christian Fellowship (formerly the Inter-Varsity Fellowship), a student
movement linking Christian Unions in universities and colleges throughout the United
Kingdom and the Republic of Ireland, and a member movement of the International
Fellowship of Evangelical Students. For information about local and national
activities write to UCCF, 38 De Montfort Street, Leicester, LE1 7GP.*

*InterVarsity Press, U.S.A., is the book-publishing division of Inter-Varsity
Christian Fellowship, a student movement active on campus at hundreds of
universities, colleges and schools of nursing. For information about local and regional
activities, write IVCF, 233 Langdon St., Madison, WI 53703.*

*Distributed in Canada through InterVarsity Press, 860 Denison St., Unit 3,
Markham, Ontario L3R 4H1, Canada.*

*Text set in Great Britain*
*Printed in the United States of America*

*UK ISBN 0-85111-833-X (paperback)*
*Library of Congress Catalog Card Number: 79-1994*
*USA ISBN 0-87784-962-5 (hardback)*
*USA ISBN 0-87784-261-2 (paperback)*
*USA ISBN 0-87784-880-7 (set of Tyndale Old Testament Commentaries, hardback)*
*USA ISBN 0-87784-280-9 (set of Tyndale Old Testament Commentaries, paperback)*

*18   17   16   15   14   13   12   11   10   9   8*
*96   95   94   93   92   91   90   89   88   87*

# GENERAL PREFACE

THE aim of this series of *Tyndale Old Testament Commentaries*, as it was in the companion volumes on the New Testament, is to provide the student of the Bible with a handy, up-to-date commentary on each book, with the primary emphasis on exegesis. Major critical questions are discussed in the introductions and additional notes, while undue technicalities have been avoided.

In this series individual authors are, of course, free to make their own distinct contributions and express their own point of view on all debated issues. Within the necessary limits of space they frequently draw attention to interpretations which they themselves do not hold but which represent the stated conclusions of sincere fellow Christians. The books of Ezra and Nehemiah have long been the subject of special and complex academic controversy, not least concerning the order of events recorded. Mr Kidner sincerely maintains the traditional order of their appearance on the stage of history of these two influential Jewish leaders at a time of great national crisis. Other views are by no means ignored; the author purposefully places detailed discussion of some aspects of them in Appendices, to enable the general reader to concentrate on the over-all teaching, message and relevance of these Old Testament books.

In the Old Testament in particular no single English translation is adequate to reflect the original text. The authors of these commentaries freely quote various versions, therefore, or give their own translation, in the endeavour to make the more difficult passages or words meaningful today. Where necessary, words from the Hebrew (and Aramaic) Text underlying their studies are transliterated. This will help the reader who may be unfamiliar with the Semitic languages to identify the word under discussion and thus to follow the argument. It is assumed throughout that the reader will have ready access to one, or more, reliable rendering of the Bible in English.

Interest in the meaning and message of the Old Testament continues undiminished and it is hoped that this series will thus further the systematic study of the revelation of God and His will and ways as seen in these records. It is the prayer of the editor and

5

publisher, as of the authors, that these books will help many to understand, and to respond to, the Word of God today.

D. J. WISEMAN

# CONTENTS

## AUTHOR'S PREFACE

I AM glad to take the opportunity which a Preface offers of making a few acknowledgments. I am grateful to Miss Ann Bradshaw for her skill in deciphering a veritable palimpsest to produce an orderly typescript; to Dr Hugh Williamson for drawing my attention to articles which I might easily have overlooked; to the Tyndale Library for providing almost all the reference material which was needed; and to the Editor of this series for giving me this absorbing task.

May this commentary not add greatly to the 'much rubbish'[1] that surrounds the city of God, but even help to stop a gap or two in its defences.

To my regret, the NIV (New International Version, 1979) came into print too late to be consulted among the other translations of the Old Testament.

DEREK KIDNER

---

[1] See Ne. 4:10.

# A SELECTION OF DATES

# CHIEF ABBREVIATIONS

| | |
|---|---|
| Ackroyd | *1 and 2 Chronicles, Ezra and Nehemiah* by P. R. Ackroyd (*Torch Bible Commentaries*), 1973. |
| *AJBA* | *Australian Journal of Biblical Archaeology.* |
| *AJSL* | *American Journal of Semitic Languages and Literatures.* |
| *ANET* | *Ancient Near Eastern Texts* edited by J. B. Pritchard, ²1955. |
| AV | Authorized Version (King James), 1611. |
| *BA* | *Biblical Archaeologist.* |
| *BASOR* | *Bulletin of the American Schools of Oriental Research.* |
| Batten | *Ezra and Nehemiah* by L. W. Batten (*International Critical Commentary*), 1913. |
| BDB | *Hebrew–English Lexicon of the Old Testament* by F. Brown, S. R. Driver and C. A. Briggs, 1907. |
| *BH* | *Biblia Hebraica* edited by R. Kittel and P. Kahle, ⁷1951. |
| Brockington | *Ezra and Nehemiah* by L. H. Brockington (*Century Bible*, New Series), 1969. |
| *BWANT* | *Beiträge zur Wissenschaft vom Alten (und Neuen) Testament.* |
| Coggins | *Ezra and Nehemiah* by R. J. Coggins (*Cambridge Bible Commentary on the New English Bible*), 1976. |
| *DOTT* | *Documents from Old Testament Times* edited by D. Winton Thomas, 1958. |
| *ET* | *Expository Times.* |
| G-K | *Hebrew Grammar* by W. Gesenius, edited by E. Kautzsch and A. E. Cowley, ²1910. |
| GNB | Good News Bible (Today's English Version), 1976. |
| Heb. | Hebrew. |
| *IDB* | *Interpreter's Dictionary of the Bible.* |
| JB | Jerusalem Bible, 1966. |
| *JBL* | *Journal of Biblical Literature.* |
| *JNES* | *Journal of Near Eastern Studies.* |
| Josephus | *The Antiquities of the Jews* by Flavius Josephus (1st century AD). |
| *JSS* | *Journal of Semitic Studies.* |
| *JTS* (NS) | *Journal of Theological Studies* (New Series). |

## CHIEF ABBREVIATIONS

| | |
|---|---|
| K–B | *Lexicon in Veteris Testamenti Libros* edited by L. Koehler and W. Baumgartner, 1953. |
| Keil | *Ezra, Nehemiah and Esther* by C. F. Keil, 1873. |
| LXX | The Septuagint (pre-Christian Greek version of the Old Testament). |
| mg. | margin. |
| MT | Massoretic Text. |
| Myers | *Ezra, Nehemiah* by J. M. Myers (*Anchor Bible*), 1965. |
| NBD | *The New Bible Dictionary* edited by J. D. Douglas, 1962. |
| NEB | The New English Bible: Old Testament, 1970. |
| OTS | *Oudtestamentische Studiën.* |
| PEQ | *Palestine Exploration Quarterly.* |
| RSV | American Revised Standard Version, 1952. |
| Rudolph | *Esra und Nehemia* by W. Rudolph, 1949. |
| RV | English Revised Version, 1881. |
| Ryle | *Ezra and Nehemiah* by H. E. Ryle (*Cambridge Bible*), 1907. |
| Syr. | The Peshitta (Syriac version of the Bible). |
| VT | *Vetus Testamentum.* |
| Vulg. | The Vulgate (Jerome's Latin version of the Bible). |
| ZAW | *Zeitschrift für die alttestamentliche Wissenschaft.* |

# INTRODUCTION

## I. EZRA AND NEHEMIAH IN THE SETTING OF THEIR TIMES

T HE chequered story of the Kings, a matter of nearly five centuries, had ended disastrously in 587 BC with the sack of Jerusalem, the fall of the monarchy and the removal to Babylonia of all that made Judah politically viable.

It was a death to make way for a rebirth. A millennium before this, Israel had been transplanted to Egypt, to emerge no longer a family but a nation.[1] Now her long night in Babylon was to mark another turning-point, so that she emerged no longer a kingdom but a little flock with the makings of a church. This is the point at which the book of Ezra begins.

Its own story can be soon told, at least in outline. It covers, with the book of Nehemiah, a little over a hundred years, from 538 BC when Cyrus sent the exiles home to re-erect their temple, to some point around 430, or in the following decade, when Nehemiah exercised his second term of office in Jerusalem.[2] It is not continuous, but centres round three movements and personalities. First there was the struggle to get the Temple rebuilt in the days of Zerubbabel (with Jeshua the high priest and eventually Haggai and Zechariah the prophets). This went on from 538 to 516, and it dominates Ezra 1-6, apart from a digression in chapter 4:6-23. Then we hear no more for nearly sixty years, when another expedition sets out from Babylonia. This time it is led by Ezra, whom the emperor has commissioned to enforce the law of Moses—a task whose immediate consequences bring the book to a painful and abrupt conclusion. The third great personality is Nehemiah, who largely tells his own invigorating story of rebuilding the city wall, of outfacing his enemies, repopulating Jerusalem and routing the traitors within his camp. By the end of these two books the former exiles have had their chief structures, visible and invisible, re-established, and their vocation confirmed, to be a people instructed in the law and separated from the nations.

But this renewed sense of identity went hand in hand with

[1] The point is forcefully made in Dt. 26:5ff.
[2] This chronology is disputed; see below, Appendix IV: A question of chronology, pp. 146ff.

political subservience. Oddly enough, they were now more distinctively themselves, more Jewish, than at any time of their existence as a sovereign state. There was now less scope for dreams of grandeur; there had been hard lessons; there were some men of steel to lead them. Providentially, too, the Persian empire gave positive encouragement to its peoples to practise their own religions in full style and with due seriousness.

This brings us to the wider setting of these books, and some brief account of this world power.

The founder of the Persian empire was Cyrus the Great, formerly king of the small state of Anshan near the Persian gulf. He had displaced his overlord Astyages in 549 BC, thereby inheriting the vast Median empire which overarched, to the north and east, that of Babylon. This he extended far to the west into Asia Minor by defeating Croesus of Lydia in 547, to the growing alarm of Babylon and Egypt, the allies of his victim. In 539 Babylon fell to him without a struggle, and he began to fulfil unwittingly the prophecies of Isaiah 44:28; 45:1ff. by re-patriating the captive cult-objects and peoples of the Babylonian empire, rebuilding their temples and asking their intercessions. An extract from his account of this on the 'Cyrus Cylinder' is given on p. 18.

In 530 Cyrus went to battle in the eastern regions, only to die and be succeeded by Cambyses, his son, who in 525, with extraordinary swiftness, added Egypt to his dominions. It is a point of interest that whereas many Egyptian temples were desecrated in this campaign a Jewish sanctuary at Elephantine, a garrison town at the southern border, was spared. (See below, pp. 17ff., on the religious policy of this dynasty.)

But before setting out on this venture Cambyses had secured his throne by having his brother Smerdis (known also as Bardes or Bardiya) murdered and the fact of his death concealed. If this was effective in the short run, it brought a crop of trouble to Cambyses' successor. Among the many rebel leaders who sprang up in all parts of the empire when the throne fell vacant in 522 were two who successively claimed to be the missing heir. Only the vast energy and skill of Darius I (521–486) availed to restore stability by the end of his second year. This was the year 520 in which Haggai and Zechariah started prophesying, and in which the work on the Temple was at last resumed,[1] as recounted in

---

[1] Some writers have detected allusions to this recent unrest and the ensuing

Ezra 5 and 6. Zechariah's two visions of horsemen patrolling the earth (Zc. 1 : 7ff.; 6 : 1ff.) may well owe something of their form to the relays of swift couriers who enabled the king's writ to run throughout his enormous realm (*cf.* Est. 8 : 10).

The next king, Xerxes I (486-465/4) or Ahasuerus (these are the Greek and Hebrew/Aramaic forms of the Persian name Khshayarshu), is mentioned only in passing in Ezra (4:6), though he dominates the book of Esther. He is memorable in world history for his spectacular but fruitless expedition against Greece in 480. His father's campaign had given the Greeks the glory of Marathon in 491; his own added the names of Thermopylae and Salamis to their history.

It is his successor, Artaxerxes I (464-423), who brings us again into substantial contact with our two books, from Ezra 7 to the end of Nehemiah (together with a mention of Darius (II) in Ne. 12 : 22[1])—though many scholars would place Ezra's career in the reign of Artaxerxes II (404-359) or even Artaxerxes III (359-338). This departure from our author's chronology is discussed at length on pp. 146-158. Assuming however that Ezra was indeed sent in 458 to regulate affairs in Judah, his mission could well have seemed politically useful to Artaxerxes I, whose early years were plagued with the revolt of Inaros in Egypt, and who would therefore have been especially anxious to promote good order in this nearby territory. A few years later (449) Megabyzus, his own governor of Syria, was to rise in rebellion. The king's sensitivity over this area is seen in Ezra 4 : 7ff., where his fears of disloyalty in Judah were easily played upon. Once again, though, he had the good sense to recognize a man whom he could trust, in appointing Nehemiah as governor of Judah in 445 and giving him a free hand.

Some light on Nehemiah's local conflicts and their aftermath comes from extra-biblical sources, from which we learn that his opponents were men of considerable status. Sanballat was, either now or later, governor of Samaria (see on the Elephantine papyri, below, p. 143), Geshem was the leader of a quite powerful group of Arab communities, and Tobiah was probably governor of Ammon and a member of an influential Jewish family. His designation as 'the servant' is probably a con-

---

calm, in Hg. 2 : 6 and (four months later) Zc. 1 : 11. See, however, J. G. Baldwin, *Haggai, Zechariah and Malachi (Tyndale Old Testament Commentaries*, IVP, 1972).
[1] Some argue that the Darius of this verse is Darius III. See below.

temptuous abbreviation of 'the king's servant'. From the Elephantine papyri we know also that by 407 Sanballat's sons, Delaiah and Shelemiah, were acting for him, and we note from their names that their father paid at least lip-service to Yahweh— a fact which must have added to Nehemiah's difficulty in opposing him. The Samaria papyri found in 1962 at Wadi Daliyeh reveal that this family was still in office and still of the same religion in the middle years of the next century, when the son of a second Sanballat was governor, bearing the Yahwistic name of Hananiah.[1]

The last king to be mentioned in the book of Nehemiah (but only in a chronological note, Ne. 12 : 22) is 'Darius the Persian', *i.e.*, evidently Darius II (423-404). In his reign the letters known as the Elephantine papyri were written, giving us a first-hand footnote to our story (see pp. 143ff.). But with the close of the century our knowledge of Jewish affairs to the end of the Persian empire in 331 fades to almost nothing—unless we take the view, which I reject, that Ezra's lifetime belongs to that period, under Artaxerxes II or III (404-359, or 359/8-338/7). There are some scraps of information, but little that is certain or significant. From some inscribed jar handles found at Ramat Raḥel it seems that Judah continued to have Jewish governors (though there are scholars who read not 'the governor' [*phw'*] but 'the potter' [*phr'*], *i.e.*, the makers of the jars).[2] Some ancient authors, including Eusebius, speaking of punitive measures against Sidon and other trouble-makers, say that Artaxerxes III deported a number of Jews to Hyrcania (near the Caspian sea) early in his reign—but they are writing many centuries after the event.[3]

What is both certain and significant is that at some point

[1] See F. M. Cross, 'The Discovery of the Samaria Papyri', *BA* 26 (1963), pp. 110-121. Josephus (*Ant.* xi. 7. 2) speaks of an apparently third Sanballat in the time of 'Darius the last king', *i.e.*, Darius III, 336/5-331, but his garbled Persian chronology and his apparent confusion of this person with Nehemiah's Sanballat make him an unreliable witness at this point. See H. H. Rowley, *Men of God* (Nelson, 1963), pp. 256f.; H. G. M. Williamson, *JTS* (NS) 28 (1977), pp. 49-66.

[2] For 'the potter' see F. M. Cross, 'Judean Stamps', *Eretz Israel* 9 (1969), esp. p. 24; also J. Naveh, *The Development of the Aramaic Script* (Jerusalem, 1970), p. 61. For 'the governor' see Y. Aharoni, *The Land of the Bible* (Burns & Oates, 1966), p. 360; also, replying to Cross and Naveh with fresh evidence, N. Avigad, *Bullae and Seals from a Post-Exilic Judean Archive* (Jerusalem, Qedem 4, 1976), pp. 6f.

[3] See, however, D. Barag in *BASOR* 183 (1966), pp. 6-12, on archaeological indications that some Jewish cities may have suffered deportations at about this time.

between Nehemiah and the second century BC (*cf.* 2 Macc. 6:2; Ecclus. 50:25f.) the Samaritans built their own temple on mount Gerizim, next to Shechem, so making the breach with the Jews almost irreparable. Josephus (*Ant.* xi. 8) places this event at the transition from the Persian to the Greek period, *i.e.*, about 330, telling how Sanballat obtained Alexander's permission to build it and to instal his son-in-law as priest. There is too much confusion here with the events of Nehemiah 13:28 (a century earlier) to make Josephus a good witness to the details; but he may be right about the time of building.

So the two centuries of the Persian empire were among the most formative periods of Jewish history. Out of the ruins of the little kingdom of Judah there had emerged the small community whose concern to be the people of God by pedigree and practice shaped it into the nation which meets us in the New Testament. Already the future prominence of the Temple and its priests, of the law and its scribes, as well as the enmity between Jews and Samaritans, could be seen developing. Throughout this time the Persian régime was given a substantial part to play, both in sending and subsidizing the three expeditions, of Zerubbabel, Ezra and Nehemiah, and in backing their authority with its own. It was not the first empire, nor the last, to be allotted some such role.

## II. THE RELIGIOUS POLICY OF THE PERSIAN KINGS

A notable feature of the Persian empire was its integration of a great diversity of peoples into a single administrative system, while maintaining at the same time a tradition of respect for their local customs and beliefs. The religion of the Achaemenid kings[1] was (at least from Darius I onwards) the worship of the one god Ahura-Mazda, but this was not imposed on peoples of other faiths. Rather, they were encouraged to seek the king's welfare by observing the proper forms of their own religions.

Cyrus, the first king, identified himself with his new subjects even to the extent of professing allegiance to Marduk and the other gods of Babylon, at the same time restoring the images of non-Babylonian deities to their former cities, repatriating their worshippers, rebuilding their sanctuaries and soliciting their

---

[1] Named after Achaemenes, royal ancestor of Cyrus, in whose family the kingship remained throughout the two centuries of the empire's existence.

patronage. The so-called Cyrus Cylinder, from which the following is an extract, gives his own account of this.

> 'I returned to these sacred cities ..., the sanctuaries of which have been in ruins for a long time, the images which (used) to live therein and established for them permanent sanctuaries. I (also) gathered all their (former) inhabitants and returned (to them) their habitations ...

> 'May all the gods whom I have resettled in their sacred cities ask daily Bel and Nebo for a long life for me ...; to Marduk, my lord, may they say this: "Cyrus, the king who worships you, and Cambyses, his son ..."'[1]

What this meant for the Jews, and so for the world, begins to be shown in Ezra 1.

Occasional glimpses of this policy at work reach us from other sources—for the grants of money and materials made to the Jews by Cyrus, Darius and Artaxerxes for the needs of worship[2] were by no means unparalleled. In Egypt, Cambyses and Darius I took Egyptian throne-names in honour of the god Re, and although Cambyses embarked at one stage on a series of temple destructions and acts of sacrilege, this action was out of character—possibly a reprisal for some suspected priestly plot, since he spared a Jewish temple in the same area. Previously he had paid the customary honours to the Egyptian gods and had strengthened the authority and revenues of the priests of the goddess Neith at his capital city. Darius likewise poured out money and labour on Egyptian religion, 'in order' (as his priestly Egyptian chronicler puts it) 'to uphold the name of all the gods, their temples, their revenues, and the ordinances of their feasts forever'.[3]

Nor was Egypt an exceptional case. The inhabitants of the Greek island of Delos, when they fled at the approach of the Persian fleet in about 490 BC, were given an assurance of Darius's veneration for so sacred a spot, the birthplace of Apollo and Artemis; and the Persian general Datis made lavish offerings there. More significantly, the same king Darius I made specific mention of a long-standing royal policy in these matters in the

---

[1] The rest is damaged. This translation is from *ANET*, p. 316.

[2] *Cf.* Ezr. 3:7; 6:4, 8-10; 7:15-24.

[3] From the inscription of Uzahor at Saïs, as rendered by G. B. Gray in *The Cambridge Ancient History*, IV (CUP, 1926), p. 25.

course of a rebuke to one of his officials in Asia Minor. The official, Gadatas, had failed to exempt certain cult-servants, the 'gardeners of Apollo', from paying tribute. The same kind of privilege, for all grades of Jewish temple officials, was written into Artaxerxes' letter of appointment to Ezra (Ezr. 7:24).

Finally, the concern of these kings to ensure that the native religions were correctly practised is illustrated in the 'Passover Papyrus' of the Elephantine texts.[1] This is a letter, dated 419 BC, from a Jewish provincial official named Hananiah to a group of Jews in the garrison of this Egyptian frontier town of Elephantine, reporting an order from Darius (II) that the local governor should authorize them to hold a festival of unleavened bread. Hananiah has evidently been charged to spell out the procedure to them, which he does in terms which summarize Exodus 12:6, 14-20. He concludes his letter with the formula, 'By order of King Darius'.

This scrap of papyrus not only forms a companion piece to the account of Ezra's commission to enforce the Jewish law, but confirms what the wording of the royal decrees in that book implies: that the broad decisions on these matters were passed on to advisers for detailed drafting; that the advisers were compatriots of the people concerned; and that the documents then went out in the king's name.

These scattered examples of Persian policy, although not essential to our understanding of the two books, enable us to see them not in isolation but in close and convincing relation to their times.

### III. SOME LEADING THEMES OF EZRA-NEHEMIAH

Quite clearly these two books are more than a bare chronicle. Here are events to learn from, not only to learn about. There is indeed a certain kinship between this last stretch of narrative in the Old Testament and the last in the New, in that both bring the reader to a point of arrival which is a staging-post rather than a destination, and tacitly invite him to explore God's purpose further. With Nehemiah at Jerusalem, just as with Paul at Rome, the narrative breaks off abruptly, leaving us in no doubt of a stiff journey ahead, but also of a venture well launched and of great potentiality. 'The hand of our God' (to borrow a favourite phrase of Ezra–Nehemiah) has been much in evidence; and since

[1] On these texts see also below, pp. 143ff.

He is the acknowledged author of these events, what is said of Him must be the first theme to study.

### a. *God*

There is no question here of a small and cloistered deity, however tiny a remnant His people have become. He is boldly acclaimed as creator and sustainer of 'heaven, the heaven of heavens, with all their host', to say nothing of the earth and all its creatures (Ne. 9:6); and this is no privately held theology. The Jews' reply to a formidable commission reporting to the emperor was: 'We are the servants of the God of heaven and earth' (Ezr. 5:11)—a title which, abbreviated to 'the God of heaven', was indeed already known to the authorities as the correct form of reference to the God of Israel (*cf.*, *e.g.*, Ezr. 1:2; 6:9). For private encouragement His people could remind one another that He was also 'great and awesome' (Ne. 4:14 [8, Heb.]; *cf.* 9:32), and that He was committed to them as '*our* God'.

There is in fact a strong emphasis on the covenant by which God had bound Himself to Israel in this way, and thereby to the individual as 'my God' (a relationship of which Nehemiah was specially conscious). His choice of Abraham, His rescue of Israel from Egypt and His patience under their provocations, dominate the great confession of Nehemiah 9 and, less broadly, of Ezra 9; and the same faithful love had sent His Spirit among them, however little heeded, in the wilderness and in the preaching of the prophets (Ne. 9 : 20, 30).

This divine steadfastness is the first thing that meets us in this pair of books. The whole train of events was set in motion to fulfil a promise (Ezr. 1:1). What is equally apparent is the divine sovereignty. There are no overt miracles, but one imperial decision after another is quietly initiated by the Lord, who 'stirred up the spirit of Cyrus' (Ezr. 1:1), 'put' a certain thing 'into the heart' of Artaxerxes, and again saw to it that 'it pleased the king to send' Nehemiah to reverse a previous policy (Ezr. 7:27; Ne. 2 : 6). Equally, of course, it was God who roused the spirit of each volunteer, we are told, to return from exile (Ezr. 1 : 5), and 'put into' Nehemiah's heart to tackle first the wall (Ne. 2 . 12) and then the living human structure which it must serve (7 : 5).

Finally, God is seen here working with as well as in His people, and against as well as through the men of power. The story of Nehemiah is famous for its marriage of the wholly spiritual with the unashamedly hard-headed. 'We prayed . . and set a guard

... against them day and night' (Ne. 4:9). 'Remember the Lord . . .and fight' (4:14). The excellent result is recorded with characteristic gratitude, making nothing of the fact that Nehemiah had outwitted the enemy, although he had, but rather that 'God had frustrated their plan' (4:15). This, after all, was the heart of the matter and the sign of greater things to come. So even the enemy perceived. When the wall was finished in a mere 52 days, the surrounding peoples 'fell greatly in their own esteem', not because they saw the Jews as disquietingly efficient, although again they were, but because 'they perceived that this work had been accomplished with the help of our God' (6:16).

If such a God were for them, who could be against them? Whether He chose to protect His people through their own vigilance and hard work, as above, or through the imperial officers and horsemen who escorted Nehemiah to Jerusalem (Ne. 2:9), or invisibly and silently, as He protected Ezra on a similar journey when he was 'ashamed to ask the king' for military help (Ezr. 8:22), the entire operation was 'the Lord's doing', and it is still marvellous in our eyes.

### b. *The people of God*

Isaiah had foretold that although Israel might be 'as the sand of the sea, only a remnant of them' would 'return' (Is. 10:22)—return, that is, not only from exile but 'to the mighty God' (21). Our two books present us with both aspects of this matter: the smallness of the remnant and a new consciousness that it was a people apart.

Even though there were nearly 50,000 who came back from exile (Ezr. 2:64ff.), these homecomers felt themselves to be only a handful by comparison with their forebears. 'We are left a remnant that has escaped' (Ezr. 9:15). But the very fact of survival was a confirmation of God's 'favour' and 'steadfast love' (Ezr. 9:8f.)—so that the term, 'the exiles', (the *gôlâ*, a collective noun) became an honourable title, virtually the equivalent of 'the true Israel'. This slips out in the proclamation of Ezra 10:8, which threatens certain defaulters with being 'banned from the congregation of the *gôlâ*', although the exile itself had ended eighty years before.

Two things were stressed in this new era: first, continuity with the historic Israel, whose name and inheritance were carried on by this remnant (*cf.* Ezr. 2:2b), and secondly, separation from the taints of heathenism. The patient recording of families and home towns in Ezra 2 reflects the first of these concerns, and this is underlined by the listing of certain groups in verses 59 and 60 which 'could not prove their fathers' houses or their descent, whether they belonged to Israel'. It was not only the priests (verses 61–63) who had to produce a pedigree.

The second concern, that of religious purity, was harder and more hazardous to pursue. It carried the dangers of the ghetto, of attracting hostility and breeding arrogance. The hostility was felt at once after the first rebuff of a dubious offer of co-operation, recorded in Ezra 4; but there is little sign of arrogance in the exclusiveness found necessary at this stage. It was still a defensive rather than an offensive stance, and in all sections of society there were many who found it irksome. Since it fell to the leaders to insist upon it, it would be possible to accuse Zerubbabel, Ezra and Nehemiah of mere chauvinism; but it would be fairer to point out that their task was to preserve the identity of Israel as 'the holy seed' (Ezr. 9:2; *cf.* Mal. 2:15), and its loyalty to the Lord as something entire and absolute, not to be swamped or diluted by the culture that encircled them.

These were crucial issues. The glimpses that we have in Ezekiel and Jeremiah (*e.g.*, Ezk. 8; Je. 44:15ff.) of popular religion at the beginning of the exile, and the further glimpses in the Elephantine papyri[1] of Jewish expatriates of Nehemiah's time who saw no incompatibility between Yahweh and Canaanite deities, show the direction which post-exilic Judaism might easily have taken. And it should be added that the dismissive verdicts on certain neighbours, 'You have nothing to do with us', and 'You have no portion or right or memorial in Jerusalem' (Ezr. 4:3; Ne. 2:20), are balanced and illuminated by the welcome given to genuine converts. The passover that marked the completion of the Temple, we are told, 'was eaten by the people of Israel who had returned from exile, and also by every one who had joined them and separated himself from the pollutions of the peoples of the land to worship the Lord, the God of Israel' (Ezr. 6:21). Conversely, a Jewish pedigree conferred no moral exemptions. Long before Paul made his memorable gesture of shaking out his garments in rejection of his faithless compatriots (Acts 18:6), Nehemiah had enacted the same dramatic warning against Jewish usurers and oath-breakers, adding 'So may God shake out every man from his house and

[1] See below, pp. 143ff.

from his labour who does not perform this promise' (Ne. 5:13). For all the emphasis of these books on externals, the way a man treated his fellows remained the test of his profession. And there is something almost Pauline again in Nehemiah's renouncing of his perquisites as governor, 'because of the fear of God' and 'because the servitude was heavy upon this people' (Ne. 5:14-19; *cf.* 1 Cor. 9:3-18).

The people of God, then, were still confronted with the ethical implications of the covenant and with calls to courageous faith such as had been given by the prophets. But the three successive foci of activity in these two books, namely, the Temple, the law and the wall, bring into special prominence the character of Israel as God's minority group in an alien world, His 'own possession among all peoples'. As such, this community was priestly: called to offer worship, not only through material sacrifices but in songs and prayers for which a highly organized temple staff was maintained (see especially Ne. 11:15-24). It was becoming, in the second place, the people of a book—not only in the sense that the Mosaic law was now vigorously enforced (especially over mixed marriages) but that it was expounded and given a major part to play in worship (*cf.* Ezr. 7:10; Ne. 8:3, 8; 9:3). With this emphasis and the example of the scholarly Ezra, the role of the scribe in Israel was already beginning to emerge in its developed form. The third focus of the story, the rebuilding of the wall, almost asks to be seen as a symbol of Israel's separatism: the material expression of a siege mentality. While this is not altogether fair, since the wall had been torn down in a campaign of slander and intimidation and rebuilt in a spirit of faith, it is true that Nehemiah used it not only for physical protection but for spiritual quarantine, to defend the sabbath from violation (Ne. 13:15-22). It is also true that separatism was now being taken with new seriousness as a demand of the law ('I . . . have separated you from the peoples, that you should be mine'—Lv. 20:26), and was thereby—not unlike the city wall itself—potentially a means either of preservation or else, if it should loom too large, of constriction.

In short, what we see in Ezra–Nehemiah is an Israel cut down almost to the roots, but drawing new vitality from its neglected source of nourishment in the Mosaic law and already showing signs, by its new concern for purity, of growing into the Judaism which we meet, both for better and for worse, in the New Testament.

### c. Means of grace

To keep the subject within bounds we must confine it to three overlapping areas: cultus, prayer and Scripture.

**1.** Under *cultus* we can take note of the regular provisions for worship. The altar was set up at the first opportunity, lest unatoned sin and neglected homage should add the displeasure of heaven to the enmity of man ('for fear was upon them because of the peoples of the lands', Ezr. 3:3). The Temple, however, lay abandoned for years, first by necessity, then by neglect, until its ruins became an affront to God and a challenge to His prophets (Hg. 1:4; Zc. 4:9). With its completion, Israel again had her visible centre and a role for the army of priests, Levites, singers, gatekeepers and Temple servants who had hastened to return from captivity (Ezr. 2:36ff.). Some idea of the colour and movement of the great occasions of worship, with instrumentalists and antiphonal singers, with the congregation's shouts of joy or lamentation and with the lurid spectacle of sacrifice, can be gained from such passages as Ezra 3:10ff.; 6:16ff.; Nehemiah 12:27ff. Even the daily services had something of this quality, with morning and evening sacrifices and with choirs which had their named leaders and responders (*cf.* Ne. 11:17, 23; 12:8f., 24). All this was intensified at the festivals, which added the dimension of a vivid commemoration of God's saving acts—whether with the passover lamb and the unleavened bread (Ezr. 6:20ff.) or with the home-made arbours that turned all Jerusalem into an Exodus encampment (Ne. 8:14ff.).

**2.** *Prayer* is woven thoroughly into the fabric of these two books. It takes a variety of forms, from a momentary flash of mental prayer to an eloquent address, accompanied on a penitential occasion by such outward gestures as fasting, pulling out the hair, rending the garments, weeping, casting oneself down (*cf.* Ezr. 9:3; 10:1), or wearing sackcloth and putting earth on one's head (Ne. 9:1); or again, on a joyful occasion reinforcing praise with the music and shouts of acclamation which we noted in the paragraph above.

In their content the prayers reflect a mature Old Testament faith. There is a strong sense of history and of Israelite solidarity, not only where this is reassuring (by virtue of election and covenant and the memory of redemption, Ne. 9:7–15) but equally where it is humiliating. Ezra blushes (Ezr. 9:6) for the guilt of the present and the past, although he has had no obvious personal share in either; likewise Nehemiah's general confession, 'we have sinned', is immediately personalized: 'Yea, I and my father's house have sinned' (Ne. 1:6); and there is no excuse offered. God is just (Ezr. 9 : 15; Ne. 9 : 33); indeed the punishment has been 'less than our iniquities deserved' (Ezr. 9 : 13).

Such self-humbling, by itself, can grow morbid. In these examples, however, the outcome is doubly healthy: not only is courage taken from the biblical promises and from the 'little' signs of God's continued love (Ne. 1 : 8f.; Ezr. 9 : 8f.), but in each case the confession leads on to costly action. Ezra 9 is followed by the drastic chapter 10; Nehemiah 1 leads into the do-or-die encounter with the king (and since the prayer looked forward to 'success . . . today' (11), we may suspect that Nehemiah knew exactly what he was doing when he allowed his air of gloom to attract the king's attention); finally Nehemiah 9 issues in the pledged reforms of the 'firm covenant'.

Prayers of request, matched to some concrete situation, are another well-marked feature of the two books. Nehemiah's opening prayer, as we noticed, grew from confession and appeal (over a period of months—see the comment on Ne. 2 : 1) into a precise plea, naming 'today' and 'this man' (Ne. 1 : 11). His next, the famous 'arrow prayer' of 2:4, had no time for words. Between them the two rather neatly illustrate the twin facts that man's responsibility is to pray a matter through with tenacity, hard thought and deep involvement, and that God nevertheless is not dependent on our fine phrases or suggestions. The other prayers of request give much the same impression. On the one hand, Ezra allowed nothing perfunctory in his company's prayer preparation for the journey from Babylonia. 'I proclaimed a fast there, at the river Ahava, that we might humble ourselves before our God, to seek from him a straight way for ourselves, our children, and all our goods' (Ezr. 8 : 21). And on the other hand there were times when little could be said beyond 'Remember the Lord . . . and fight', or, 'Now . . . strengthen thou my hands' (Ne. 4 : 14; 6 : 9). The very brevity of these prayers is eloquent.

This brings us finally to the 'asides' of Nehemiah, mostly in the form, 'Remember me . . .' (Ne. 5 : 19; 13 : 14, 22, 31). Sometimes it is 'Remember *them* . . .', that is, the sworn enemies, the defeatists and the traitors (Ne. 6 : 14; 13 : 29); and on one occasion the prayer against them is elaborated into an imprecation: 'Turn back their taunt upon their own heads . . . Do not cover their guilt . . .' (Ne. 4 : 4f.). The affinity of this with certain psalms may give us the clue to both kinds of interjection, positive and negative. Nehemiah is committing himself and his opponents to the verdict of God. In other words, he is looking beyond success or failure, beyond the measures he is taking and must take against the opposition; beyond even the verdict of history. To have God's ready help, and, above all, God's 'well done', is his hunger and thirst and the direction of his praying. It is not surprising that his book closes with this prayer.

**3.** *Scripture*, and more precisely, the law of Moses, is the third outstanding means of grace in Ezra–Nehemiah. Other parts of the Bible are of course referred to; the whole story opens with a fulfilled prophecy of Jeremiah, and we are soon hearing well-known words from a psalm (Ezr. 3:11); but the driving and directing force is the law.

We discuss elsewhere (pp. 158-164) the theory, widely held, that this potent influence was partly due to novelty: that Ezra came from Babylon with a Pentateuch[1] larger and more elaborate than anything known before, thanks to the labours of priests and scholars like himself, who had (it is suggested) collected and modified the laws and traditions derived from various centres in Israel and blended them with the books already known, ascribing to Moses a host of material that had grown up since his day but was thought to represent his teaching or its legitimate development.

This is not a view which I share, nor is it needed (as I see it) to account for the phenomena of Ezra–Nehemiah which are our present concern. While our data could largely be explained along the lines of the last paragraph, they can also be accounted for in the light of the book of Malachi, which gives a revealing picture of the kind of religious scene which confronted the two reformers, and is generally considered to belong to approximately their period. It was a situation that called for the measures which they introduced, and its chief cause was the failure of the priests to teach the law.[2] The great impact of Ezra's law book was thus comparable in its cause and its effect to that of the Bible at the Reformation and owed its power not to its being new, but precisely to its being old and rediscovered, brought and expounded to the whole people, and treated as an authority which judged the very priests themselves (*cf.*, *e.g.*, Ezr. 9:1ff.; 10:1ff.;

---

[1] *I.e.*, the first five books of the Bible, also known by the Heb. term for law or authoritative teaching, the Torah (*tôrâ*).

[2] Mal. 2:6-9; *cf.* 3:7; 4:4. The word translated 'instruction' by RSV, *etc.*, in 2:6-9 is *tôrâ*, 'law', on which see the previous footnote.

Ne. 8: 1ff.).

An apocryphal story in 2 Esdras 14 makes Ezra a second Moses, hearing God's voice from a bush and receiving the task of writing down in forty days, with the help of five secretaries, ninety-four books, of which twenty-four (*i.e.,* the books of the Old Testament, as traditionally enumerated) were to be made known and the rest kept secret. What this fantasy embroiders is the fact that Ezra gave to Judaism its new attitude to Scripture, and so in a sense gave Scripture to the people. At last the injunctions of Deuteronomy 6: 6 began to be taken seriously. Indeed Scripture became a book to study so minutely that in the end, paradoxically, it could scarcely be seen for scribes, or heard for learned comments (*cf.* Mk. 7: 1–13; Lk. 11: 52; Jn. 5: 39ff.).

Meanwhile, however, Ezra had set a much-needed example of the right kind of biblical expertise, summed up in the famous words of Ezra 7: 10 in which a dedicated study is seen hand in hand with personal obedience and with teaching. The fact that to him the Torah, for all its legal force, was far more than a lawyer's text, comes out in a revealing word for it in 7: 25 (*cf.* 7: 14): '*the wisdom of your God* which is in your hand'. That was the king's phrase, but we need have little doubt that it reflected the attitude of Ezra.

Scripture is seen, then, in these two books as law to be obeyed and as revelation to be understood; to which we should add: as promises and warnings to evoke prayer and action. Its aspect as *law* is emphasized by the phrase 'those who tremble at the commandment' (Ezr. 10: 3; *cf.* 9: 4; 10: 9) and by the sanctions, both human and divine, which reinforced it (Ezr. 8: 26; 9: 14). As *revelation,* it was read 'clearly' (for the possible implications of this see the commentary on Ne. 8: 8), 'so that the people understood the sense'—and there was a team of teachers to make sure of this (Ne. 8: 7f.). It was also studied by laymen and priests together in what can only be described as a seminar or study-group (Ne. 8: 13). As *material for prayer and action,* we can note its use in the confessions of Ezra 9 and Nehemiah 9, and more happily in the confident reminders of God's mercy in those chapters and in Nehemiah 1. In the latter especially, the actual words of ancient promises are quoted and appealed to.

So Scripture emerges as a means of grace which, while it does not displace either the cultus or private prayer (but rather enriches and informs them), attains none the less a new prominence at this time. It was never to lose it.

27

# EZRA

## Ezra 1 – 6

## A TEMPLE FROM THE RUINS

The greater part of this book, though it bears the name of Ezra, tells of the pioneers who came back from exile to Jerusalem a whole lifetime before him. We shall not meet Ezra till chapter 7. By then, some eighty years of settling into the old country will have gone by, and he will come as a consolidator and reformer; not a temple builder like his predecessor Zerubbabel, nor a rebuilder of city walls like his younger contemporary, Nehemiah.

First, then, in chapters 1-6 we read of what awaited the earliest homecomers from Babylon: how they attempted to carry out the commission to build a new Temple; how they ran into local opposition and gave up the attempt for nearly twenty years; how they rallied at last and completed it, against a background of threats and political manoeuvres. The threats were defied, the manoeuvres were self-defeating, and this part of the story ends on a high note of rejoicing.

More than half a century was to separate that first climax from the events of chapter 7, but an earlier digression (4:6-23) will have filled in enough of the picture to show us that the Jews meanwhile continued to be bitterly resented by their neighbours; enough, too, to prepare us for the devastating opening to the book of Nehemiah.

Apart from that foretaste, the present group of chapters, Ezra 1-6, covers a single generation, 538–516 BC, and is concerned with one great enterprise, the rebuilding of the house of God: a theme which it shares with two of the prophets of the day, Haggai and Zechariah.

### Ezra 1. Liberty!

#### 1:1-4. Word from the King
**1.** This opening verse has the characteristic solidity and depth of biblical history writing, with its interest both in the external details of an event and in opening up its inner meaning. The event is datable (538 BC), and can take its place among the new policies that flowed from the fall of one empire and the rise of another. But while Cyrus had his own good reasons for what he

31

did (see below), the Lord had His; and these were, as ever,[1] the heart of the matter and the key to the future.

It was the Lord, we learn, who *stirred up* Cyrus to act, as He would also stir a group of exiles to respond (5). It was the same Lord who, unknown to Cyrus, had already 'stirred' him,[2] years before, to begin his march across the world, and had smoothed his road to victory with exactly this in view. His most significant achievement, against all human reckoning, was not to win an empire but 'to build my city and set my exiles free' (Is. 45 : 13).

More than this, God had given His *word* to Judah that the exile would be over in a mere seventy years, 'to give you', as He said, 'a future and a hope' (Je. 25 : 12f.; 29 : 10f.).[3] And God was better than His word. It was barely fifty years since 587 BC, the year when Jerusalem had fallen. There had been a deportation before this (597), and a token one as far back as 605 (2 Ki. 24 : 10–17; Dn. 1 : 1ff.), but even the longest of these spans fell short of the allotted seventy years. It was not the last time that God's mercy would shorten the days of trial (Mt. 24 : 22).

So a *proclamation* was made. This (if it followed the normal pattern) would be shouted by heralds in the principal towns of the empire, and possibly placarded as well.[4] But whether or not the *writing* was on public view, it was preserved in the records, together with administrative details for the implementing of the decision. How much was to hang on this fact would emerge twenty years later in the events of chapter 6.

**2, 3.** The famous Cylinder of Cyrus throws an interesting light on this decree. The inscription (see p. 18) tells of his allegiance to Marduk, the chief god of Babylon, and of his respect for the gods of his subject peoples. Whereas their images had been treated as trophies by his predecessors, he now restored them to their 'sacred cities', rebuilt their temples and repatriated their worshippers. He expressed the hope that these gods would

---

[1] Some classic statements of this providential control can be found in Gn. 50 : 20; Is. 10 : 5ff.; Acts 2 : 23; 3 : 17f.; 4 : 27f.; 13 : 27.

[2] See Is. 41 : 25; 45 : 13, which use this Heb. word. See also Is. 44 : 28 – 45 : 7 for Cyrus's unconscious fulfilment of God's role for him.

[3] Daniel remembered this and prayed for its fulfilment. He was rewarded with a vision of this pattern repeated on a grander scale and with finality (Dn. 9 : 2, 24ff.). Also in 520 BC, with the exile over but the Temple unbuilt, Zechariah heard the angel pleading for an end to 'these seventy years' of wrath, and being promised that 'my house shall be built . . .' (Zc. 1 : 12–17).

[4] *Cf.* E. J. Bickerman, 'The Edict of Cyrus in Ezra 1', *JBL* 65 (1946), pp. 249ff. (especially 272–275).

therefore pray for him daily to the gods of Babylon: Bel, Nebo and above all, Marduk.

From his own standpoint, then, to have the house of *the God who is in Jerusalem*[1] rebuilt was but one instance of a consistent policy. More than one of his successors would show the same concern for correct religious protocol (see pp. 17ff.). The homage paid in verse 2 to the Lord was doubtless a diplomatic courtesy, yet sincere enough in its way. It was important to frame the decree correctly for each repatriated group, and *the God of heaven* was how the Jews described their deity. Moreover to a polytheist of Cyrus's wide sympathies it would seem clear that all the gods had willed his triumph; therefore each in his proper context could be thanked for it.

According to Josephus, however (*Ant.* xi. 1), Cyrus had been shown the prophecy of Isaiah 44:28, which names him, and was eager to fulfil it. While this is not impossible,[2] it has no corroboration; and Cyrus's own inscription shows that any knowledge he may have had of the Lord was nominal at best. Isaiah 45:5f. insists that to know the Lord involves acknowledging no god beside Him.

**4.** To a devout Jew there were two expressions here to quicken his interest. One was the word for *survivor*, which in Hebrew would call to mind Isaiah's insistent message that 'a remnant' would return (*cf.* Is. 10:20ff.). The other was an echo of the Exodus, in the call to the neighbours of the pilgrims to speed them on their way with *silver and gold* and other gifts, just as the Egyptians had done centuries before (Ex. 12:35f.). It would chime in with Isaiah's songs about a second Exodus (Is. 43:14ff.; 48:20f., *etc.*), which lifted the whole enterprise on to the highest level.

Besides these voluntary gifts there were to be payments and releases from the royal treasury, specified in a separate document which found its way into the royal archives. This record was to play a vital part in a later crisis, as recounted in chapter 6; meanwhile the safe return of the Temple vessels forms the climax of the present chapter.

---

[1] The end of verse 3 can also be punctuated as in AV, RV, making 'he is the God' a self-contained interjection. But this is somewhat awkward, and LXX, Vulg. and the massoretic punctuation support the interpretation adopted by RSV, *etc.*

[2] Bickerman indeed sees it as quite probable: 'The Jews would hardly abstain from quoting these revelations in approaching Cyrus, nor would he neglect the divine voice. Josephus may be right . . .'. Bickerman, *art. cit.*, p. 269.

## 1:5-11. Treasures to Jerusalem

**5.** Nearly two hundred years after the kingdom of Israel had disintegrated, the remains of the little kingdom of Judah, which had always included some members of the other tribes,[1] still had some cohesion and could rightly bear the name of Israel (*cf.* 1:3b; 2:2b). Now the Lord, as though to emphasize that He is not the God of the big battalions,[2] stirred only a remnant of this remnant into action. This whittling down of numbers and power, ever since the heyday of the kings, is reminiscent of His way with Gideon's army and, later, with the crowds of Galilee and Judea. But the more obvious emphasis is on the word *stirred*, echoing what was said of Cyrus in verse 1, to make it doubly clear that this enterprise was from the Lord. Otherwise, as Psalm 127 shows, the builders and the watchmen would have done their work in vain.

**6.** On this echo of the Exodus story, see on verse 4. That verse shows also that the term *freely offered* refers to gifts for the Temple itself, the rest being evidently meant for the pilgrims. There was no question, incidentally, of their refusing this money from unbelievers; rather, as Haggai 2:7f. would point out, since the treasures of all nations were the Lord's, they were His to command.[3]

**7.** In the absence of images to restore as in the case of other religions (see on verses 2-4), the Temple vessels, or articles (the word is very general), made an obvious substitute. The written order for their return, and for the Temple's rebuilding at the royal expense, is preserved in 6:1-5.

**8.** The names of the two officials give us a glimpse of the new and the old régimes now combined. *Mithredath* is a Persian name in honour of Mithras the sun god ('Mithras has given'),[4] and the word that describes him as *treasurer* is also Persian. The name *Sheshbazzar* on the other hand is probably connected with the conquered nation's sun god, the Babylonian Shamash.

Sheshbazzar is better described as chief or (NEB) 'ruler' than as *prince*, for the Hebrew word carries no necessary implication of royal descent. The question of his identity is discussed

---

[1] *Cf.* 2 Ch. 11:1-4, 13-16.
[2] *Cf.* Zc. 4:6, 10, spoken to this generation.
[3] It was another matter when a gift came explicitly from a corrupt practice (Dt. 23:18) or might be reckoned to give the donor the status of a patron (Gn. 14:23).
[4] There is another Mithredath in 4:7. It was quite a common name; its Greek form Mithradates is more widely known.

in Appendix II, pp. 139ff. There is a view that Sheshbazzar
was a second name for Zerubbabel, used in all transactions
with the ruling power (*cf.* other re-namings, *e.g.*, 2 Ki.
24:17; Dn. 1:7). Alternatively Sheshbazzar and Zerubbabel
may have been, respectively, the official and unofficial leaders of
the enterprise. Neither view is without its difficulties.

**9-11.** From this prosaic inventory (and the textual problems
it now presents to us—see 'Additional note' below) it is left to us to
picture what it may have meant to see this consecrated gold and
silver brought out into the light of day, every piece of it a witness
to God's sovereign care and the continuance of the covenant.
The political kingdom had perished, but not the 'kingdom of
priests'. The businesslike transfer of articles, 'counted out' (8)
from one custodian to another, may have been outwardly
undramatic, but it was momentous. The closing words of the
chapter, *from Babylonia to Jerusalem*, mark one of the turning-
points of history.

### Additional note on the list of vessels, 1:9-11

There are obscurities here in both the vocabulary and the
figures. Basins (*'agartᵉlê*) is a loan-word, a fact which may mean
that the author was using an inventory compiled by a foreigner
(*cf.* perhaps the archives mentioned in 6:1ff.). *Censers* (*cf.* 1
Esdras 2:13) is one of many guesses at the Hebrew *maḥᵃlāp̄îm*. RV
has 'knives', LXX 'changes' (of raiment? *i.e.*, priestly robes?). The
word does seem to derive from √*ḥlp*, to change, but probably
means either 'duplicates' or 'varieties' (*cf.* NEB).

The problem of the figures is that in the Hebrew text
(supported by LXX) the separate items add up to less than half the
recorded total. Therefore RSV (unlike AV, RV, JB, NEB) follows
the tidier figures of 1 Esdras 2:13f. (see RSV mg. for the details).
In defence of the Hebrew text one might argue that the
named items are only a selection; but verse 10b mentions 'a
thousand other vessels', which should take care of the remainder.
So it seems that either the total or the components have been
misunderstood (if signs were used for the numerals), or
miscopied.[1] There may be a pointer to textual damage in the

---

[1] On the signs used for numerals see H. L. Allrik, *BASOR* 136 (1954),
pp. 21-27. On discrepant totals, D. J. Wiseman refers (in a written communication) to 'the well-known fact that some lists are excerpts, though they still keep
to the original totals for the whole list (*e.g.*, as in Alalakh texts)'.

Hebrew word *mišnîm* (10), whose normal meaning, 'double' or 'second', is not compellingly relevant here.[1] It is thought by many to be the remains of a numeral. I Esdras 2 : 13, adopted by RSV, has 'two thousand' at this point.[2] These are speculations; but few commentators doubt that the author was drawing on an actual list, whose original form showed the completeness of the hand-over of Temple vessels.[3]

### Ezra 2. The pilgrims

This chapter, however uninviting it may seem, is a monument to God's care and to Israel's vitality. The thousands of homecomers are not lumped together, but (in characteristic biblical fashion) related to those local and family circles which humanize a society and orientate an individual. Such is God's way, who 'setteth the solitary in families' (Ps. 68 : 6, AV, RV). And for the people's part, their tenacious memory of places and relationships, still strong after two generations in exile, showed a fine refusal to be robbed of either their past or their future.

So these were living portions of Israel, roots and all, for re-planting. But the fundamental motive for this careful grouping was not social but religious. This is the holy nation, given a new chance to live up to its calling. There can be nothing casual in its preparations. Not only must every priest have his credentials (61–63) but every member too (59f.), whether as a true-born Israelite or as belonging to a constituent household (65) or guild (*cf.* 43–58)—or again (as we learn later, 6 : 21) as a convert. It was something more than antiquarianism which would impel Nehemiah, nearly a hundred years later, to make this long catalogue the check-list for his regrouped community, and to reproduce the whole of it in his memoirs (Ne. 7 : 5–73).

The final paragraphs show another aspect of Israelite vitality (68f.) and another glimpse of a structured community which had a well-marked variety of components (70) and a God-given centre of unity (3 : 1).

---

[1] RV has 'of a second sort' – but where is the first sort? NEB more plausibly sees it as a synonym of *maḥ*ᵃ*lāp̄îm* ('of various types').

[2] Torrey, cited by Batten, conjectured that the consonants *mšnym* were all that remained of *'lpym šnym*, '2000'. Batten objects that 2000 is regularly written as the dual *'alpayim* without the numeral. In an unvocalized text, however, the numeral would be by no means superfluous.

[3] 2 Ki. 24 : 13b appears to leave no vessel intact in 587 BC; but from Dn. 5 : 2ff. and from our passage it is clear that the objects that were cut up were not the smaller pieces, but presumably everything that was too big to transport whole.

## 2:1, 2a. The leaders

The section headings below will show how orderly an account, group by group, this chapter gives of the return. For its general interest, see the paragraph above; the notes that follow are mostly on minor points of detail.

**1.** *The province* (*m'dînâ*) in question is Judah, a small district within the great administrative area known as Beyond the River, *i.e.*, Syria and Palestine (see on 4:10). Judah was perhaps carved out of adjacent districts and newly granted an identity of its own—for Sheshbazzar was arriving there as governor (*cf.* 5:14). If so, the ruffled feelings of officials shorn of part of their command may have helped to set the hostile tone which they and their successors tended to adopt. And at the local level the collective word used here for *exiles*, the *gôlâ*, was to become something of an irritant, as a term which marked off the community that had been through its ordeal in Babylon from the rather suspect multitude that had escaped that purging.

**2a.** There are eleven names here, but Nehemiah's copy of the list preserves one more, that of Nahamani (Ne. 7:7), which has evidently dropped out of this verse in the course of copying. The choice of twelve, like that of the twelve apostles, was a tacit declaration that the community they led was no mere rump or fragment but the embodiment of *the people of Israel* (note the final words of this verse) and the corporate inheritor of the promises. Compare the reminder of the Exodus noted at 1:4, and the offering of 'twelve bulls for all Israel' in 8:35.

*Zerubbabel*, a grandson of king Jehoiachin,[1] was the natural leader of such a company, whether his position at this stage was official or unofficial.[2]

*Jeshua* the High Priest (Zc. 3:1), whose name (in Greek, 'Jesus') is spelt Joshua in Haggai and Zechariah, was Zerubbabel's fellow-leader. So close, indeed, was this partnership that it was seen by Zechariah as the foretaste of the perfect régime to come, when priesthood and royalty would unite in one man: 'the

---

[1] He is known as the son of Shealtiel (3:2, *et al.*) who was Jehoiachin's eldest son. But the Heb. text of 1 Ch. 3:19 makes Zerubbabel the son of Pedaiah, who was a younger brother of Shealtiel. If this is the true text, it implies a levirate marriage of Pedaiah to the widow of Shealtiel, whereby the firstborn was reckoned as Shealtiel's to keep the family name in being (*cf.* Dt. 25:5f.; Ru. 4:10). As Shealtiel's heir, he would be first in line for the throne.

[2] It was certainly official by the time of Haggai (Hg. 1:1). On the question of his relationship to Sheshbazzar see Appendix II, below, pp. 139ff.

man whose name is the Branch'.[1]

Some of the remaining names may look familiar to us, but time and place rule out their identification with the well-known Nehemiah or Mordecai, or with Seraiah the father of Ezra, or the Bigvai of Nehemiah 10:16.[2] It is just that such names were common in this general period.[3]

## 2:2b-35. The lay Israelites

Two ways of identifying and 'placing' a person are here. Some Israelites had records of a recognized family or clan (3-19 or 20), others knew their traditional home town (20 or 21-35). An appendix to the list will mention people whose standing was in doubt (59f.), and even these are shown in groups according to their settlements in exile and their families. To be rootless and anonymous was the last thing an Israelite could wish to be.

A comparison of this list with Nehemiah's copy of it (Ne. 7:7bff.) reveals a startling contrast between the transmission of names and that of numbers—for the names in the two lists show only the slightest variations[4] whereas half the numbers disagree, and do so apparently at random. The fact that the two kinds of material in the one document have fared so differently lends the weight of virtually a controlled experiment to the many other indications in the Old Testament that numbers were the bane of copyists. Here the changes have all the marks of accident. Now one list, now the other, will give the larger figure, and the

---

[1] Zc. 6:11-13, where AV/RV is the most faithful translation. See J. G. Baldwin, *Haggai, Zechariah and Malachi, ad loc. Cf.* Je. 23:5 for 'the Branch' (*ṣemaḥ*), or 'shoot', as a Messianic title.

[2] Another bearer of this name, differently spelt, is Bagoas, the governor of Judah *c.* 410 BC, mentioned in the Elephantine papyri. See further, pp. 145f.

[3] Some commentators have suggested that we have here the well-known Nehemiah, *etc.*, and that therefore the list either betrays the confused inventiveness of a late redactor (so Kellermann, *Nehemia: Quellen, Überlieferung und Geschichte, Beihefte zur ZAW* 102 (1967), p. 99; *cf.* the confusion in 1 Esdras 5:8, 40, where this Nehemiah is appealed to as an arbitrator or governor), or that it combines successive waves of immigration. It is pointed out that in Ne. 7:7 the equivalent of Seraiah is Azariah, a name similar to Ezra. This is fragile material for a hypothesis, which is not strengthened by the further supposition that the Mordecai here is Esther's uncle, turned pilgrim in the end.

[4] The only substantial difference is the absence of *Magbish* (30) from Ne. 7. There are two changes of order: Ezr. 2:17 and 19 are transposed in Ne. 7:22f., and Ezr. 2:33f. in Ne. 7:36f. *Jorah* (Ezr. 2:18) becomes Hariph in Ne. 7:24, and *Gibbar* (20) becomes Gibeon in Ne. 7:25 (raising the question whether this name marks the last of the clans or the first of the towns in the chapter).

differences will range from units to many hundreds.[1] On the totals, see on verse 64.

## 2:36-39. The priests

These numbers add up to 4,289: about a tenth of the pilgrim company. King David had organized the priests into twenty-four family groups to take turns of duty; but only four of these were represented among the homecomers, and the same four families are still the only ones mentioned in 10:18-22, several generations later. So it was from these four, according to the Tosephta (ii. 1, 216), that the twenty-four duty rotas were reconstituted, adopting the names of David's original groups.[2]

Wellhausen gratuitously assumed that the *Jeshua* whose 973 descendants are mentioned here (36) was the high-priestly Jeshua of these chapters (though this is not stated here, and there is another unidentified Jeshua in verse 40); therefore the narrator was allegedly taking his figures from a very late list[3] and failing to notice what he was implying. The natural sense of the verse, however, is similar to that of verse 40, where a family's or clan's subdivisions are marked by pivotal names from its earlier history.

*Pashhur* (38) is a name not found in 1 Chronicles 24, but may indicate the surviving branch of the Malchijah group, if 1 Chronicles 9:12 refers to the Malchijah of 1 Chronicles 24:9. Both Pashhur and Malchijah, however, were names common enough to make identifications precarious. *Cf.* the two together in Jeremiah 38:1, and two others in Jeremiah 20:1; 38:6.

## 2:40-42. The Levites

As with the priests, it was only a minority of Levites who returned at this stage. While all who are mentioned in these three verses were of the tribe of Levi, the term *Levites* in verse 40 probably means those who directly assisted the priests, as against

---

[1] There are 'single figure' differences in the parallels to verses 6, 10, 11, 13, 17, 33; a difference of 1100 at verse 12; and various anomalies in between. These are informatively discussed in the light of the contemporary signs used for numerals in H. L. Allrik, 'The lists of Zerubbabel (Ne. 7 and Ezr. 2) and the Hebrew numeral notation', *BASOR* 136 (1954), pp. 21-27.

[2] The names are given in 1 Ch. 24:7-18. For their persistence, *cf.* 1 Ch. 24:10 with Lk. 1:5.

[3] J. Wellhausen, 'Die Rückkehr d. Juden a.d. Bab. Exil', *Nachrichten der königl. Gesellschaft der Wissenschaften zu Göttingen* (1895), p. 177.

those who belonged to the guilds of verses 41f., whose origins are described in 1 Chronicles 25:1 - 26:19.

Here an interesting shaft of light falls, quite incidentally, on the antiquity of the Mosaic law and its freedom from later interference. For now the Levites, whom the tithe law treats as greatly outnumbering the priests, had suddenly become a tiny minority with only a fraction of their former claim on the community's support. Yet the law gives them everything, 'every tithe in Israel', and only requires them to hand on a tenth of this to the priests: 'a tithe of the tithe' (Nu. 18:21, 26). Had the law been still in the making or rewriting at this stage, as many have tried to argue, it could never have reached us in this form. To quote Y. Kaufmann, who draws attention to this:

'Nothing proves more clearly how mistaken is the view that in post-exilic times, the Torah book was still being added to and revised. ... The founders of post-exilic Judaism were not the composers, but merely the collectors of the Torah literature. They did not alter anything of what they "found written", much less add to it.'[1]

## 2:43-54. The Temple servants

We are told in 8:20 that David and his officials had founded this order of assistants to the Levites. Their Hebrew name is the Nethinim (*nᵉṯînîm*), as RSV margin points out, meaning the 'given' or 'dedicated' ones, which is a variation on one of the descriptions of the Levites themselves, of whom God said 'they are wholly given (*nᵉṯûnîm*) to me.'[2]

It seems likely that the more menial tasks fell to these men; and the presence of some foreign-looking names in the list[3] may indicate that some of these groups came into Israel from David's conquests, whether as immigrants or perhaps as prisoners of war. Certainly there were foreign units in his army (2 Sa. 15:18-22), and from an earlier stage (though for a different reason) the Gibeonites had been enrolled in Israel as a labour corps (Jos. 9:27).

---

[1] Y. Kaufmann, *The Religion of Israel* (Allen & Unwin, 1961), p. 193.

[2] Nu. 8:16.

[3] *E.g.*, in other OT contexts, Rezin (48; *cf.* Is. 7:1) and Sisera (53; *cf.* Jdg. 4:2); also the apparently tribal plurals Meunim and Nephisim (50; *cf.* 1 Ch. 4:41 and the Ishmaelite Naphish of 1 Ch. 1:31). Several other names suggest a non-Israelite origin by their form or by their occurrence in foreign records. For details, see the larger commentaries.

Not long before the events of this chapter Ezekiel had preached against the use of 'foreigners, uncircumcised in heart and flesh' as sanctuary attendants (Ezk. 44:6–8), and some have seen in this an attack on the Nethinim. He may have had certain Nethinim in mind, but not the Nethinim as such, for his attack is on those who are resolutely alien, who refuse the obligations of the covenant. Exodus 12:48 makes it clear that if a non-Israelite family accepted circumcision, the covenant blessings were all theirs (*cf.* Nu. 15:14f.). Had there been any doubt about the Nethinim in principle, they would have found no place in this chapter.

### 2:55-58. Descendants of Solomon's servants

This group is closely linked with the previous one, and a single total serves for the two of them in verse 58. This fact suggests that Solomon may have recruited them to supplement David's Nethinim, but for secular tasks. Samples of their kinds of employment, or those of their forebears, may be preserved in the words *Hassophereth* ('the scribe', 55) and *Pochereth-hazzebaim* ('the gazelle-keeper', 57).[1] The only other mention of this community is in the parallel passage (Ne. 7:57ff.) and in Nehemiah 11:3, where again it is named just after the Nethinim.

### 2:59, 60. Unconfirmed claims: (a) of Israelite birth

The place-names seem to be those of the captivity, though they are unidentified as yet.[2] The importance of family records was twofold: for settling claims to property, and for ensuring that the restored community had an unbroken descent from the original Israel. But it was not pressed beyond this point: the unsuccessful claimants were not sent back, but evidently given provisionally the same standing as the circumcised foreigners, whose rights we have already noticed in the comments on verses 43–54.

Yet for all its value in preserving the chosen people, this emphasis on a pure Israel had considerable dangers, as the New Testament shows by its attacks on those who preened themselves on their pedigree. Presumably the Christian has his own form of

[1] Both these titles are feminine in form, like the word Qoheleth (for the author of Ecclesiastes) which is used with masculine predicates. The form appears to denote an office or office-bearer.

[2] The prefix *Tel-* means a mound such as is formed by the growth of a town on its successive layers of occupation. Ezekiel's Babylonian place of exile was Telabib (Ezk. 3:15), but the term Tel- was also used in Palestine: *cf.* Jos. 11:13.

this temptation, and his own lesson to draw from the Pauline aphorism: 'they are not all Israel, which are of Israel'.[1]

## 2:61-63. Unconfirmed claims: (b) to the priesthood

The fate that overtook Korah and his company when they tried to force their way into the priesthood was a standing reminder to Israel of the peril of such a course: 'so that no one who is not a priest, who is not of the descendants of Aaron, should draw near to burn incense before the Lord' (Nu. 16:40). Therefore the precautions that were now being taken were not excessive but a plain duty.

**61.** *The sons of Hakkoz* evidently had their claim upheld in the end, if Ezra's contemporary, 'Meremoth *the priest*, son of Uriah' (8:33), was the same person as 'Meremoth the son of Uriah, *son of Hakkoz*' in Nehemiah 3:4, 21. Against this it could be urged that the Meremoth of Nehemiah 3:21 appears to be classified with the Levites of verses 17ff.; but it is not stated how far that list extends, and in fact Meremoth's colleagues on either side were apparently priests. See footnote on Nehemiah 3:17ff.

*Barzillai* was a name that carried considerable weight: its bearer had been a staunch supporter of David, and a man of wealth (2 Sa. 19:32). It may be that in adopting this family's name (and becoming its heir?) the ancestor of these claimants had laid himself open to the charge that he had renounced his own birthright, the priesthood. It was laid down as part of the cost—and reward—of being a priest that (as God told Aaron) 'You shall have no inheritance in their land, neither shall you have any portion among them; I am your portion and your inheritance ...' (Nu. 18:20).

**63.** The word here for *the governor* is the Persian term Tirshatha, which AV, RV retain in this verse and in its four occurrences in Nehemiah (7:65,70; 8:9; 10:1).[2] Here it evidently refers to Sheshbazzar (*cf.* 5:14, using the commoner word *peḥâ*, which is Assyrian-based). His identity is discussed on pp. 139ff. Here it is interesting to note that he and not the high

---

[1] Rom. 9:6, AV. *Cf.* Rom. 2:28f.

[2] Attempts at finding an etymology for Tirshatha have yielded meanings as diverse as 'excellency' (from a Persian verb 'to tremble'; hence, questionably, 'inspirer of awe'), or 'eunuch' or 'circumcised' (the two latter deduced from a modern Persian verb 'to cut'). See W. Th. In der Smitten, '"Der Tirschātā" in Esra-Nehemia', *VT* 21 (1971), pp. 618-620. But safer guides than etymology are synonyms (*cf. peḥâ*, used of Sheshbazzar, Ezr. 5:14, and of Nehemiah, Ne. 5:14) and contexts; and these point to the familiar translation, 'governor'.

priest had to settle this ecclesiastical question. Whether the *Urim and Thummim* (through which the answer might otherwise have come[1]) had been lost in the exile, or whether the ability to use them had been withdrawn, is not entirely clear; but the latter seems to be implied by the wording of the sentence. *Cf.* Psalm 74:9, 'We do not see our signs; there is no longer any prophet, and there is none among us who knows how long.' There are two occasions also in 1 Maccabees (4:46; 14:41) when decisions had to be postponed for lack of revelation. Heaven seemed to have fallen silent, though in the present case the silence would soon be broken by prophecy again (5:1).

### 2:64-67. The totals

**64.** The figure of 42,360 appears as the total also in Nehemiah 7:66 and 1 Esdras 5:41, yet the individual items add up to three different totals, as follows: Ezra, 29,818; Nehemiah, 31,089; 1 Esdras, 30,143. There have been attempts to explain the missing thousands: as members of the northern tribes, or as women, or as adolescents.[2] But the narrative is silent on such points. As regards the northern tribes, it has made no distinction between them and Judah in the classified lists above, for those groups of homecomers are seen there as men of 'Israel' (2:2b, 59), not of a tribal minority.[3] As regards women, would the men in these family groups have outnumbered them by well over two to one? And the mention of the age of twelve and upwards in 1 Esdras 5:41 would have needed to be contrasted with an adult age in listing the separate groups (as Keil points out), had the author of 1 Esdras meant to reconcile the figures by his insertion of this phrase. There is general agreement that the divergences are copying errors, arising from the special difficulty of understanding or reproducing numerical lists. On this, see the second

---

[1] See Ex. 28:30; Nu. 27:21. In the light of the longer text (Greek) of 1 Sa. 14:41 (as in RSV, NEB, *etc.*) it is suggested that the Urim and Thummim may have been a pair of small objects whose obverse or reverse sides signified God's 'Yes' or 'No' if both objects showed the same side uppermost when the high priest drew them out of their receptacle. God's refusal of an answer (1 Sa. 28:6) was perhaps indicated by a failure of the two to coincide. Josephus (*Ant.* iii. 8. 9) asserted that the answer was given by a miraculous shining of the jewels on the high priest's breastplate or shoulder-piece, but that this had long since ceased.

[2] 1 Esdras 5:41, which seems to raise this possibility, excludes children under twelve from its grand total.

[3] There were members of other tribes than Judah in the restored community (1 Ch. 9:3) but not, as far as we know, on this scale.

paragraph of comment on verses 2b–35, above. See also on the next two verses.

**65.** This inordinate number of slaves (rather than 'servants'; *cf.* NEB), about one to every six freemen, agrees with the evidence of wealth in verse 69, and makes the subsequent poverty described by Haggai less than twenty years later an object-lesson on material insecurity. A run of bad harvests and high prices (Hg. 1 : 6, 9ff.; 2 : 17), to say nothing of enemy intervention (Ezr. 4), would soon leave nothing but their expensive houses (Hg. 1 : 4) to remind them of their former well-being.

The *singers* were distinct from the temple choirs of verse 41 and were simply a pleasant addition to a wealthy establishment: *cf.* 2 Samuel 19 : 35.[1]

## 2:68, 69. The gifts

*Freewill offerings*, such as are mentioned here and at 3 : 5, are a sign of health in any enterprise, and all the more so when an official grant offers a temptation to complacency (if 'grant' is the right translation in 3 : 7, as I think it is). The phrase, *according to their ability*, does credit to these donors, and Paul may have had it in mind in his charge to the Corinthians to give in proportion to their gains (1 Cor. 16 : 2); perhaps, too, in his admiration of those who had given not only 'according to' their ability but, paradoxically, 'beyond' it (2 Cor. 8 : 3).

The parallel passage, Nehemiah 7 : 70–72, is more detailed at this point, mentioning separately the contributions of the governor, of some heads of houses, and of the rest of the people; also listing some of the offerings in kind, rather than in monetary terms.[2] In this connection it is worth noting the valuation in Ezra 8 : 27 of 'twenty bowls of gold worth a thousand darics'.

[1] At this point the copy of this list in Ne. 7 provides a text-book example of one source of scribal errors ('*homoioteleuton*'). There the copyist's eye has travelled from the *two hundred* (which in Heb. follows the word *singers*) to the same word in the next verse, where it is followed by 'forty-five'. So in Ne. 7 : 68 the intervening words are missing from the Heb. text (though inserted in the mg. of some MSS), leaving the singers' number as 245 and omitting the mention of horses and mules. See RSV mg. at Ne. 7 : 68. It illustrates again the hazards surrounding such lists, already noted above.

[2] The various sets of figures can be totalled as follows:

|              | Ezr. 2:68f. | Ne. 7:70–72   | 1 Esdras 5:45 |
| ------------ | ----------- | ------------- | ------------- |
| Gold darics  | 61,000      | 41,000        | 1,000         |
| Silver minas | 5,000       | 4,200 (4,700?) | 5,000        |
| Vessels      | —           | 50            | —             |
| Garments     | 100         | 597 (97?)     | 100           |

## 2:70. Settlement in the towns

The words (lived) *in Jerusalem and its vicinity*, are borrowed from
1 Esdras 5:46 by RSV and most modern versions, on the
assumption that they have dropped out of the present text by
accident. The copying of this chapter was clearly an arduous
task, as we have seen, and the mention of Jerusalem as the home
of the priests and Levites and some others makes excellent sense.
There would soon be daily sacrifices to offer, many worshippers
to attend to, and much work to supervise (3:4ff.).

## Ezra 3. Altar and Temple

### 3:1-6a. First things first

It would have been easy to rest content with the bare fact of
arrival and resettlement in the homeland. But there was the
king's business—the Temple—to attend to; and prior to even
that, there was the basic calling of Israel. That vocation, like
ours, was to be 'a holy priesthood, to offer spiritual' (and in their
case, literal) 'sacrifices acceptable to God'.[1]

So the first thing to be built was the altar (2), before even the
materials were ordered for the Temple (7). Abram had marked
his arrival in the land in just such a way, setting up his altar as a
bold Amen to the promise (Gn. 12:7). But these settlers were
moved as much by fear as by faith: *fear . . . because of the peoples of
the lands* (3). This could be taken to mean that they dared not
attempt anything so ambitious as a Temple; but in view of verse
7, which sees them putting that work in hand, it is more likely to

---

The two figures in parentheses reflect the fact that the words 'five hundred' in Ne.
7:70 (69, Heb.) are oddly placed, indicating that an item (silver minas?) has
dropped out of the text, leaving this floating '500' evidently attached to the
wrong object.

The word variously translated 'darics' or 'drachmas' is *darkeᵐônîm*. If 'darics'
(RV, RSV) is correct, the author is evidently expressing the amounts in terms of
the coins of his own day, since these were apparently introduced by Darius I
(521-486), a later king than Cyrus. The Greek drachma (JB, NEB) was not current
in Palestine for another 200 years. An alternative suggestion (see H. Hamburger
in *IDB, s.v.* Daric) derives the Heb. word from a much older term, the Assyrian
*darag mana* (= ¹⁄₆₀ of the mina). This term, however, is not attested in the Assyrian
dictionaries and is doubtful, since ¹⁄₆₀ of a mina would be a shekel.

The gold daric, of which a few examples survive, weighed a little more than
the British golden sovereign. The silver mina (Heb. *māneh*), appropriately
rendered 'pound' (weight) in AV, RV, is reckoned to have weighed 500 grams (1.1
lb) and was worth 60 shekels; but there were 'common' and 'royal' as well as
'light' and 'heavy' versions of these units.

[1] 1 Pet. 2:5; *cf.* Ex. 19:6.

imply that the threatening situation had brought home to them their need of help, and therefore of that access to God which was promised at the altar. 'There', He had said, 'I will meet with the people of Israel' (Ex. 29 : 43).

It also made them careful over detail. The altar was set *in its place* (3), *i.e.*, its traditional and proper place; and we read of all being done *as it is written . . . as it is written* (2, 4), even to the elaborate numerical sequence of offerings at the feast of booths (4), which takes twenty-seven verses to describe in the book of Numbers (Nu. 29 : 12–38). So the system of offerings and festivals was set in motion, beginning on the day which ushered in the seventh month (6) with trumpets (Lv. 23 : 24), the month which was the climax of the Jewish year. It was a worthy start to the new era. It had the backing of the whole people, who *gathered as one man to Jerusalem* (1), and whose leading family, that of Zerubbabel, joined with the priests in setting up the altar. But the initiative on this occasion rightly belonged to Jeshua, whose name precedes Zerubbabel's only here (2).

### 3:6b–9. Preparations for the Temple
To lay the foundation is one meaning, but not the full range, of this single Hebrew word which can cover the whole process of making a structure fit for use—a job which here would include the work of carpenters as well as masons, and which in 2 Chronicles 24 : 12ff. meant the repair of a building which was by no means in ruins. In verse 10 it obviously describes the first stage of all, but in Haggai 2 : 18 it marks the resumption of this work after many years' neglect.[1]

**7.** In the transaction with Sidon and Tyre there is an echo—perhaps a conscious imitation—of Solomon's preparations for the first Temple. He too had had the timber sent by sea to Joppa, and had paid for it with the country's natural exports of grain, wine and oil (2 Ch. 2 : 10, 15f.), which could presumably be loaded onto the returning ships. All this was now made possible not only by the gifts recorded in 2 : 68f. but by the *grant*[2]. . . *from Cyrus* (which is mentioned here for the first time), for the new settlers would not yet have any produce of their own to export. It was a tiny foretaste of the 'wealth of the nations' and

---

[1] On the implications of this, see Appendix II, p. 140.
[2] *Grant* is found only here, and basically means permission. Since permission to buy materials would hardly need specifying, it is reasonable to take the word to include provision as well as permission, as with our own word 'grant'

'the glory of Lebanon' which it was promised would flow in one day 'to beautify the place of (God's) sanctuary' (Is. 60:11, 13).

**8, 9.** It was fitting, again, that the work should start in *the second month* of the new year, for the first was dominated by the Passover. Besides—and this would hardly have escaped their notice—the second was the month in which Solomon's Temple had been started (1 Ki. 6:1).

The careful planning and recording of the operation are impressive. There was enthusiasm, reflected in the 'all' who came forward for the work (8b), but there was strict attention to standards, as is shown by the double mention of *the oversight*: first of *the work* (8), secondly of the *workmen* (9). Evidently the Levites as a whole[1] supervised the work of the laymen, and were themselves directed by their leading families (9).[2]

### 3:10-13. Climax and anticlimax

So the crescendo continues, to the strange close of the chapter. Once again, there are conscious echoes of Solomon's celebrations, though there are contrasts too. This time there is no ark, no visible glory, indeed no Temple: only some beginnings, and small beginnings at that. But God is enthroned on the praises of Israel, and these could be as glorious as Solomon's. Perhaps they were more so, for while they matched the earlier occasion, word for word and almost instrument for instrument (2 Ch. 5:13), they were sung in conditions more conducive to humility than to pride, and called for a faith that had few earthly guarantees to bolster it.

The last two verses have all the unexpectedness of actuality. The spontaneous cry of disappointment, breaking into the celebrations, was a foretaste of much that was to follow. Haggai

---

[1] The qualifying age for service varied with the times, the nature of the work and perhaps the numerical strength of the tribe. For the carrying of the sacred vessels on the march it had been 30 (Nu. 4:3ff.); for the general tabernacle service, 25 (Nu. 8:24); here and in 1 Ch. 23:27 (but see 23:3) and 2 Ch. 31:17 it was 20.

[2] Brockington points out that the term for workmen (9) can designate officials (Ne. 2:16; Est. 3:9; 9:3), *i.e.*, in this case probably the levitical foremen. A less probable meaning is that the rank and file Levites were in charge of the technical aspect of the work, while the named families were responsible for discipline.

Of the names in verse 9, the families of Jeshua and Kadmiel headed the list of Levites in 2:40, and the name Hodaviah appears there instead of Judah, probably correctly (the two names are somewhat alike in Heb., and the familiar Judah would easily slip into the text). For the family of Henadad, found again with this group, see Ne. 10:9 (10, Heb.).

would recognize that note and preach against it (Hg. 2:3ff.); Zechariah would have to challenge those who 'despised the day of small things' (Zc. 4:10). But both those prophets did so with such memorable words that we can be grateful that they had to meet this mood and answer it.

### Ezra 4. Confrontation

From this point onwards right to the end of Nehemiah there is conflict. Nothing that is attempted for God will now go unchallenged, and scarcely a tactic be unexplored by the opposition. This chapter describes the opening of hostilities and the first long set-back to the work; but before it tells of the immediate sequel, it pursues the theme of slander and intrigue well into the next century, up to the moment of disaster which was to bring Nehemiah hurrying to Jerusalem. If we were following only that theme we could go straight from verse 23 to the news of it in Nehemiah 1; but great things had been happening in the meantime, and verse 24 recalls us to the point which the narrative had reached in verse 5, before the digression.

Without that foretaste of history to reveal the full seriousness of the opposition, we should not properly appreciate the achievements recorded in the next two chapters (5 and 6) nor the dangers hidden in the mixed marriages which Ezra would set himself to stamp out (chapters 7–10). So the digression is important and functional; it is only misleading if one ignores the careful notes of time which plot the course of these events and finally return us to our point of departure, ready for the next chapter. It needs only the modern device of brackets, opening at verse 6 and closing after 23, to make this clarity doubly clear. They are well worth inserting.[1]

### 4:1-5. An offer refused

**1.** It is easy to overlook or play down the description of this

---

[1] Despite the way the passage opens (see on verse 6), the author is sometimes represented as having imagined that the events of verses 6–23 and the reigns of Xerxes and Artaxerxes all took place in the decade between Cyrus and Darius. But the rest of his book shows that he could neither have believed this himself nor wished his readers to do so. To insist on taking him in such a way is to make him not simply ignorant but totally inconsequent: one who starts by denying everything he is about to say. Only the hardest of evidence, certainly not a bare supposition, could support so odd a conclusion. See further on verses 6, 7, 12, 23, 24.

deputation as *the adversaries* and so to form an impression of the encounter as a rude rebuff to a sincere and friendly gesture. Instead, we are meant to see it as the opening of a battle of wits: the first round in an assault on the integrity of the nation-church, an attempt which would be pressed home with every kind of tactic, disarming or menacing, defamatory or obstructive, but always geared to the one objective.

In passing, we can note the mention of *Judah and Benjamin*, the two tribes which, with Levi, had been the nucleus of the southern kingdom (2 Ch. 11 : 12f.). A sprinkling of members of the other tribes had also thrown in their lot with them from time to time (*cf.* 2 Ch. 30 : 11, 18; 34 : 9). The expression, *the returned exiles*, is literally 'the sons of the captivity' (*bᵉnê ha-gôlâ*): see on 2 : 1.

**2, 3.** The mention of the *king of Assyria who brought us here*[1] provides a pointer to the story of 2 Kings 17 : 24ff., and another angle on the speakers and their religion. That story, in brief, tells of foreign communities who were forced to settle in the depopulated land of Israel after the fall of Samaria. To teach them 'the law of the god of the land' an Israelite priest was eventually sent to them, but the outcome was only a mixture of religions: 'they feared the Lord but also served their own gods'. The passage sums up bluntly what that really meant: 'To this day they do according to the former manner. They do not fear the Lord . . .' (2 Ki. 17 : 34).

Such, then, is the uncompromising verdict of Scripture on the claim *we worship your God as you do*, when it is put forward as a multi-faith proposition.[2] It was clearly the underlying reason for the Jews' reply, though they left it unsaid, contenting themselves with a flat refusal and a reference to the emperor's instructions. The refusal is expressed almost in the form familiar to us from the

---

[1] Esarhaddon (681–669) began his reign 40 years after the fall of Samaria, but the transplanting of populations was evidently a long-standing policy. It was still being practised in the next reign, that of Ashurbanipal (the Osnappar of verse 10). Verse 10 also shows that what is told of 'the cities of Samaria' in 2 Ki. 17 was not confined to a small area, but affected the rest of the province.

[2] There is a small textual difficulty behind the words *we have been sacrificing to him*, since the Heb. has 'not' (*lō'*) instead of 'to him' (*lô*). MT and virtually all versions treat this as a scribal error. The two words sound alike, and are confused in several places (notably Is. 9 : 3a, where AV awkwardly retains 'not'). Here, the word-order favours 'to him'; so does the tone of the request. Conceivably, 'we have not been sacrificing' could imply 'because we had no temple'; but since all that was needed for sacrifice was an altar (*cf.* 3 : 6) it would have been an irrelevant remark.

49

Gospels, 'what have we to do with you?', except that here it is a statement. NEB puts it well: '(it) is no concern of yours'.

**4, 5.** The resulting campaign of harassment by the local people[1] had the double force of persistence (the Heb. has a string of participles: they kept doing these things) and of variety. Discouragement (4a) relies on the subtle weapons of suggestion and sneers; intimidation (4b) and threats. Not content with these, they must get their victims discredited and on the wrong side of the authorities—and they were prepared to buy professsional help (5) to achieve this.

It is small wonder that they succeeded. The supply-lines from Lebanon (3:7) were long and vulnerable, the new community felt exposed and surrounded; besides, as Haggai's preaching was to reveal, the excuse to postpone something as expensive and burdensome as building the house of God was rather tempting (*cf.* Hg. 1:2ff.). For about sixteen years, to 520 BC, the pressure against them was kept up, and as verse 24 will show, it was wholly effective.

### 4:6-23. A parenthesis: further persecutions
Any idea that the Jews had overestimated their enemies is soon dispelled by this glimpse of things to come (see the opening remarks on this chapter, above), however true it may have been that they had underestimated God.

**6.** *Ahasuerus*, familiar to us from the book of Esther, is the Hebrew form of the Persian name Khshayarsha, whose Greek form is Xerxes. This was evidently Xerxes I (486-465). The mention of him here marks simply the passage of time, which had still not cooled the enemy's antagonism. But evidently nothing came of this attempt.

**7-23.** *Artaxerxes* I reigned from 464 to 423, and was the king whose reign (in my view[2]) spanned the events of Ezra 7 to the end of Nehemiah. These complaints to him, and their outcome, show not only the dogged persistence of Israel's enemies, but the uncertainty of a great king's patronage—for this was the king

---

[1] The term, 'the people of the land' (*'am-hā-'āreṣ*), is general enough to take its meaning from its context, though it eventually became a standard term for the common and ignorant. Here it means the local population in general, whose hostility was either expressed or whipped up by the group encountered in verses 1-3. In Hg. 2:4, equally naturally, it means the rank and file of the Jewish community.

[2] Alternative views are discussed on pp. 146ff.

who had taken the trouble to send Ezra the reformer to Jerusalem. There also comes to light the delicacy of Nehemiah's task, in that it entailed obtaining a reversal of the king's policy; and we are allowed to see in verse 21 the providential loophole which left room for such a change.

**7.** This verse, to judge by the new set of names in verse 8, is most probably self-contained, simply mentioning (as verse 6 did) the sending of a letter but giving no details of it. In that case verses 6-23 tell of not two but three separate complaints, the last of which succeeded. *Bishlam* was read by LXX as 'in peace', which the consonants would allow; hence NEB has 'with the agreement of Mithredath,[1] Tabeel ... wrote to him'. This may well be right, as there is no 'and' between these words. The expression, 'in Aramaic', is repeated at the end of the verse (see RSV mg.), probably to announce the change of language[2] which now supervenes.

**8ff.** Not only this letter and the reply to it, but everything as far as 6:18 is written in Aramaic; so too is 7:12-26. On suggested reasons for this, see pp. 135f.

The repetitiveness of the next few verses comes partly from the current style of letter writing (where the words 'and now' [10c, 11c] are the equivalent of a signal to start a new paragraph), and partly from the author's decision to reproduce the high-flown preamble to the letter (9, 10) as well as his own narrative framework (8, 11a). NEB gives it a more modern lay-out, showing verses 9 and 10 as this preamble ('From Rehum...' *etc.*), 11a as the editor's note, and then 11b and 12ff. as the address and main text.

**9, 10.** The long list was calculated to impress, as were the fulsome tributes to the tyrannous Osnappar (Ashurbanipal,[3] 669-627), who, like his predecessors, had uprooted whole

---

[1] On the name Mithredath see on 1:8. This man was evidently a Persian official whose backing would be useful. Tabeel is an Aramaic name, presumably of a local leader; *cf.* another 'son of Tabeel', in a context involving Aramaean intrigues, Is. 7:6 (discussed in W. F. Albright, 'The Son of Tabeel (Isaiah 7:6)', *BASOR* 140 (1955), p. 35).

[2] Alternatively the double mention of Aramaic (omitted in RSV text but referred to in the mg.) may indicate 'Aramaic script and the Aramaic language' (JB) or the written and spoken word (*cf.* NEB). The word for 'translated' is the source of the word 'Targum', which originally denoted the oral translation of the scripture portion into Aramaic after its formal reading in Heb. in the synagogue. Hence NEB: 'and read aloud in Aramaic'.

[3] The form in which his name appears here (Osnappar) is discussed by A. R. Millard in *JSS* 21 (1976), p. 11.

populations (*cf.* verse 2). The epithets *great and noble* bring to mind the biting comments on such titles in, respectively, Luke 22:25f., Isaiah 32:5-8. But the writers of the letter are not concerned with such niceties as truth: only with exerting pressure by claiming to speak for the whole *province*[1] and to fear for the safety of the realm (*cf.* 13-16).

**12.** *The Jews who came up from you* would be Ezra's party of 458 BC (see chapters 7ff.), or else a later group. In either case some years would have elapsed before they could have been ready for the concerted building operation which provoked this letter, after the upheavals and heartbreaks of Ezra's reforms. Everything points to a date approaching the year 445 in which Nehemiah heard the news which (as I see it) corresponds to our verse 23 (Ne. 1:3).

It should hardly need emphasizing that the *walls* and *foundations* are those of the *city*, not the Temple; but the two operations are often confused. By the reign of Artaxerxes the new Temple had been standing for half a century; we shall be brought back to its story in chapter 5.

The show of touching loyalty continues, reinforced by the writers' allusion to eating *the salt of the palace* (14), *i.e.*, to considering themselves personally bound to the king by the sacred ties of hospitality. But to the reader familiar with the Jews' precarious situation there is irony in this exaggerated posture of alarm, with its crescendo from the shocked contemplation of tax evasion (13) to that of a Jewish take-over of the whole vast province west of the Euphrates (16).

**17-23.** Still more surprising is the official reaction: a classical product of research (19) without intelligence. The great days of David and Solomon (20), and even of their most spirited successors, belonged clearly to a vanished era. But there is a gleam of good sense in the last clause of 21: *until a decree is made by me.* It made a policy review possible and with it, by the grace of God, the mission of Nehemiah. The decree also forestalled to some extent, as it happened, the reproach of inconsistency over its repeal, for it had authorized only the halting of the work, not

---

[1] The term, *Beyond the River* (Aram. *ʿabar naharâ*; Bab. *Eber-nâri*; Heb. *ʿēber ha-nāhār*), is used invariably as a name, *i.e.*, 'Transeuphrates', not a descriptive phrase. The word 'province', supplied in some translations, is not present in the original. This large area, covering the whole of Syria-Palestine, was administered by a provincial governor, or satrap, under whom were governors of such districts as Samaria, Judah, Ammon, *etc.* See, further, on 5:3.

the demolition and burning which actually took place (Ne. 1 : 3). By overstepping their instructions the provincial authorities only weakened their position.

### 4:24. The narrative resumed
The word '*Then*' would at first sight point us to the verse immediately before this; but it only makes sense, as we have seen (p. 48), if it is picking up the thread of verse 5 which was dropped for the long parenthesis (6–23). The time is again that of Zerubbabel, finishing with the same phrase as in verse 5, *the reign of Darius the Persian*; but we are now told what the earlier statement stopped short of saying: first, that the work was not only hindered but halted, and secondly in what year of Darius the deadlock was broken.

### Ezra 5. The courage to rebuild

Like every spiritual advance, from Abraham's to the missionary expansion in Acts, this venture began with a word from the Lord. And in common with the rest, it was quickly tested and threatened. This chapter and the next will show what came of it, and will round off the first part of Israel's post-exilic story.

### 5:1, 2. God breaks silence
Happily we possess the very words of *Haggai and Zechariah*, and can see in their books not only the fascinating contrast between the two prophets (Haggai the plain speaker, who dots every 'i', while Zechariah is provokingly enigmatic and visionary) but also the persistence and aptness of their preaching as the enterprise wore on. Behind the simple words, *with them . . . , helping them* (2), there is more than meets the eye: four years of intimate involvement and bracing support.

We should also not miss the gentle reminder of man's accountability and heaven's help in the expression, 'God . . . *who was over them*', at the end of verse 1.[1] These workers were not on their own, in either sense of that expression.

---

[1] The clause in italics, however, represents a single Aramaic word, which might mean simply 'to them' (*cf.* AV and, by its silence, NEB), *i.e.*, '(they prophesied) to them'. But this would add nothing to what has been said, and the word in question stands as far as it can from the verb 'prophesied', which is the first word of the Aramaic sentence.

## 5:3-5 Official misgivings

The intervention came as soon as it was clear that the builders were in earnest. It was understandable. The empire had been seething with revolt throughout the first two years of Darius's reign; and now came this local burst of activity. Why were these *huge stones* (8) thought necessary? Was this simply a Temple, or something more? It was clearly the provincial governor's duty to find out, once his attention had been drawn to it. No doubt the local opponents of the work had hastened to inform him.

There is a mention of *Tattenai's* name (probably) and office (certainly) in a Babylonian record dated 502 BC which speaks of 'Ta-at[-tan-ni] governor of Ebernari'[1] (*i.e.*, of *Beyond the River*). Judah would have come under his jurisdiction, together with the whole of Syria and Palestine, and he appears to have been responsible to a still higher official named Ushtani who was over the combined satrapy of Babylon and Ebernari. *Shethar-bozenai* is assumed to have been Tattenai's assistant, and the *associates* are spoken of in verse 6 as 'governors' or 'inspectors' (NEB).[2] It was a formidable company.

The demand for credentials and, above all, *names*, portended fresh hazards. Credentials had certainly existed but might well be untraceable after so many years; and names taken down could be hostages to fortune. But *the eye of their God* upon them was better than fortune, and the integrity of the leaders evidently showed through well enough to make any immediate action other than a report seem uncalled for. What God's word had set in motion (1 : 1) had, as ever, no lack of His care, His watchful eye, to see it through. At this stage only fear could have halted the work.

## 5:6-17. The report to Darius

As a good historian, the author gives us first-hand material wherever possible: here as in 4 : 11 *the copy* of the correspondence; similarly in 1 : 2-4 and 6 : 2-5 material from the archives; later, vivid extracts from the memoirs of both Ezra and Nehemiah.

**6.** On the terms, *Beyond the River* (*i.e.*, west of the Euphrates)

---

[1] See A. T. Olmstead in *JNES* 3 (1944), p. 46; A. F. Rainey, 'The Satrapy "Beyond the River"', *AJBA*. I.2 (1969), pp. 51-78.

[2] The word (found only here and at 6 : 6) is '*ᵃparskāyē*', to be distinguished from *peḥâ* ('governor') in verse 3. It seems to be of Persian origin, but so far nothing is known of the duties of such officials. It may even have meant simply 'Persians' (*cf.* BDB), though few would support this meaning today.

and *the governors*, see on verse 3.

**8.** The expression, *the Great God*, as used by an outsider, probably meant no more than 'their chief God'. As we noticed earlier (on verses 3-5), the *huge stones* aroused suspicion of an ulterior motive for the project. The mention of *timber . . . laid in the walls* shows that Solomon's method of building was being followed (1 Ki. 6:36; *cf.* Ezr. 6:4 which prescribes the same ratio of stone to timber as Solomon's). Courses of timber at intervals, between those of stone or brick, were quite a common constructional feature over a long period in the ancient Near East, and may have originated as a means of strengthening buildings against earthquakes.[1]

**11, 12.** The title of God in these two verses would have had a familiar ring to Darius, who was a zealous worshipper of Ahura Mazda, 'the God of heaven'. But it does not follow that the Jews were being diplomatic in using such a phrase, as though to imply that *the God of heaven* could be worshipped under many names and styles. That issue had been settled for them.[2] If anything, their use of so great a title for their God was a challenge rather than a concession, and verse 12 makes sure that the exile is seen as no defeat for Him, but an exercise of power.

**14.** The identity of *Sheshbazzar*, a vexed question, is discussed on pp. 139ff. The present verse is our means of knowing of his appointment as *governor* (*pehâ*),[3] the position held now by Zerubbabel (Hg. 1:1).

**16.** Only here do we have Sheshbazzar named as inaugurating the abortive building project of chapter 3. The absence of his name from that chapter can be explained either by his having played only a formal part in the proceedings, or by the theory that Sheshbazzar was an alternative and official name for Zerubbabel, in which case it would be the right name to search for in the archives (*cf.* verse 17).

**17.** It is a small confirmation that we are reading an actual copy of the letter (*cf.* 6a), that it requested a search of records in *Babylon*, whereas the information turned out to be lodged elsewhere, as the next chapter will show.

---

[1] See H. C. Thomson, 'A Row of Cedar Beams', *PEQ* (1960), pp. 57-63, to which Ackroyd draws attention at 6:3-5.

[2] See, *e.g.*, Is. 42:8; 43:10f.; 44:6-8; 45:5-7, 22-25.

[3] Ezr. 1:8 ('prince', *nasî*) by itself might have meant no more than that he was the leading member of the Jewish community; and 2:63 does not put a name to the governor.

## Ezra 6. The Temple completed

This chapter will bring the story of the first twenty-odd years of the Return to a satisfying conclusion, rounding off what we know of the age of Zerubbabel and Jeshua. A new age, that of Ezra and Nehemiah, will open in chapter 7, a lifetime away from these events.

### 6:1-5. The decree of Cyrus rediscovered

The vastness of the Persian empire and the delays which its great distances could impose are well illustrated by this enquiry initiated in Palestine, referred to Babylon, and eventually answered from records in the remote *Ecbatana*.[1] Whatever the outcome might be, the builders had meanwhile the chance to press on, and they made good use of it.

E. J. Bickerman[2] has won general acceptance for his argument that the Hebrew proclamation in Ezra 1:2ff. and the Aramaic *record* or 'memorandum' (NEB) in 6:2c-5 have all the marks of authenticity and are 'not two variants of the same record but two independent records concerning the same case'.[3] The former was for heralds to announce (and posters to confirm, 1:1b) to the exiles whom it concerned; the latter was a 'minute' for official reference, defining the administrative details implied in the decision. Similar memoranda, noted on various kinds of writing material (*cf. a scroll*, verse 2), have been recovered from several centres in the old Persian empire. Here, in answer to Tattenai's enquiry, only matters that concern the Temple and its vessels are transcribed out of what may have been a longer document.

**4.** The *great stones* which had excited suspicion were now found to be expressly authorized—for the term is the same as for the 'huge stones' of 5:8—literally stones for rolling, too massive to be transported by other means. As for *the cost . . . paid from the royal treasury*, this was not a quixotic gesture so much as a logical implication of the project, which was prompted by the desire to win the goodwill and intercessions of whatever deities Cyrus 'repatriated' (see on 1:2-4). There could be no better use of

---

[1] E. J. Bickerman, 'The Edict of Cyrus in Ezra 1', *JBL* 65, pp. 249-275, points out (*ibid.*, p. 251) that Cyrus had stayed at Ecbatana in the summer of his first year as king of Babylon, the year in which he made this decision (1:1).

[2] See footnote 1, above.

[3] *Ibid.*, p. 250.

public money; besides, the charge on the royal revenue could be collected in the province concerned, as Darius did not fail to point out (8f.). The burden would not be felt at the capital.

**5.** The release of the Temple *vessels* was recorded in 1:7-11. Here, the instruction to restore *each to its place* is a fresh detail, which chimes in with Cyrus's concern for divine favour which we have just noted. It went without saying that worship, to be acceptable, must be correct at every point. Darius would wholly share this view, and would accept its further implications by providing the materials of 'pleasing sacrifices' and by requesting priestly intercession for the throne (9f.). The due practice of the local religions would in fact continue to be a concern of Persian policy,[1] and would have some far-reaching consequences in that it led eventually to the reforming mission of Ezra, the subject of the remaining chapters.

### 6:6-12. Darius authorizes the work

No outcome could have been more favourable, or a more striking instance of the truth which William Cowper has captured in the lines,

> 'The clouds ye so much dread
> Are big with mercy . . .'

—for the king's reply now put the Temple builders in a far stronger position than before. It gave Zerubbabel all the benefits of state money and protection, without the profaning touch of state interference.

**8, 9.** On the use of public funds, both initially (8) and subsequently (9), see on verse 4 as to the probable motive and the means of it. From the accurate list of materials for worship (9) we can gather that Jewish advice was sought in drafting the decree; and this is confirmed by the accurate theology of 12a (whereby God is seen to dwell in His Temple not by necessity or by a kind of physical presence, but by *His name*—that is, by choosing to reveal Himself there (*cf.* Dt. 12:5; 1 Ki. 8:27-29).

**11.** One who *alters* the edict would probably have included anyone who violated it (*cf.* Ryle). There was poetic justice intended in making a man's own house his instrument of execution for tampering with the house of God. The form of punishment may or may not have been impalement (RSV; *cf.* GNB's elaboration of the theme); certainly this hideous practice was no novelty, as

---

[1] See Introduction, pp. 17ff.

Assyrian monuments show. But the Aramaic reads literally 'and lifted up he shall be smitten upon it', which NEB takes to mean 'fastened erect to it and flogged', while BDB understands it as some form of crucifixion,[1] and I Esdras 6:32 as hanging. The common ground between such punishments was the public spectacle they afforded for disgrace and warning. It is a relief to know that Israelite law put two crucial restraints on such a practice: the victim was executed before this, not by means of it (Dt. 21:22; note the sequence), and the display of his corpse must not be prolonged (Dt. 21:23).

Whether the offender's house was to *be made a dunghill* or to *be forfeit* (NEB) is another open question, as NEB margin points out both here and at Daniel 2:5; 3:29.[2]

The forceful terms that enliven the king's despatch are worth extracting to make their own impact. With regard to outside interference: *Keep away; let . . . alone.* Supplies? *In full and without delay; whatever is needed; day by day without fail.* Legal sanctions? *With all diligence.* The political motives for this forthrightness may have been many, including a desire to show respect for the policies of Cyrus and to promote stability in a part of the empire which was important for communications with Egypt, at a time when widespread unrest had only recently been quelled.

But behind all this there were bigger issues than imperial politics, and better security for Israel than a king's good sense. God's 'frowning providence' (to quote again from Cowper), in allowing the opposition to raise the alarm, had not simply concealed His 'smiling face': it had given a fresh impetus to events by evoking the faith and courage of the builders and releasing a truly royal flow of material help.

---

[1] *I.e.*, it takes 'smitten' to mean 'nailed'. Myers, without committing himself to this view, notes that according to Herodotus, Darius had 3,000 Babylonians crucified when he occupied the city. Ryle draws attention to the technical meaning which the word 'lifted up' acquired (in addition to its ordinary sense) as a term for 'impaled' or 'crucified', and points out the possible bearing of this on our Lord's enigmatic use of such language in Jn. 12:32 ('I, when I am lifted up . . .').

[2] LXX, here and at I Esdras 6:32, takes the Aramaic *newālî* to mean forfeit (to the king). An Arabic root, *wly*, may support this (*cf.* Brockington), but 'dunghill' or 'ruin' can find endorsement rather nearer home, in post-biblical Heb. and Judaeo-Aramaic. The LXX in Dn. takes the similar word *newālî* to mean destruction.

**6:13-15. On to completion**

**13.** The expression, *with all diligence*, is something of a keynote in these chapters, expressing first the way the builders tackled their work (5:8), then the urgency of the king's decree (6:8, 12),[1] and finally the thorough co-operation of the civil power (6:13). *Tattenai*, as provincial governor, had acted responsibly throughout, in making the enquiry, waiting for confirmation (5:5), and giving full effect to the decree. He was no Sanballat.

**14.** We paused at 5:1, 2 to notice the seminal role of the two prophets, whose words brought a dead situation to life and two quiescent leaders into faith and action. Now the scene gains depth and momentum as we are shown *the elders*, the lesser leaders, taking up the work and pressing on to finish it, while in the background are the successive kings with their *decrees*, and at the apex the *command* (or decree[2]) *of the God of Israel*. It is a model of the way God works and of the means He uses.

The mention of Artaxerxes, who belongs to the next century, takes us forward to the restoration of the city walls by Nehemiah, which this king authorized. His name, as the third royal patron of Israel's rehabilitation, is added here to complete the picture, whether by the author or by an early scribe.[3]

**15.** The Temple was finished by the last month of 516,[4] only four-and-a-half years after Haggai's first call to action. So this venture of faith, begun in hard times (Hg. 1:6-11) and continued in a 'day of small things' (Zc. 4:10) and of ominous investigations (Ezr. 5:3ff.), ended in triumph. It was also— though nothing is made of this here—roughly seventy years since the destruction of Solomon's Temple (*cf.* Zc. 1:12-17).

---

[1] 'In full' (6:8, RSV) is a variant translation of the same Aramaic word. Note also 7:17, 21 and (RSV 'strictly') 26. In royal decrees, however, it seems to have been almost a matter of formal emphasis.

[2] The only distinction between the *command* (*ta'am*) and the *decree* (*t⁽ᵉ⁾ēm*) is the artificial change of vowels made by the Massoretes as a reverential gesture. LXX uses the same word for both; likewise AV, JB; *cf.* GNB.

[3] It was already in the text used by the Greek versions. GNB creates a contradiction by inserting in verse 14 the word 'Temple' ('They completed the Temple') where the Aramaic leaves room for the glance ahead to Artaxerxes by its more general terms ('They finished their building'), before returning explicitly to the Temple in verse 15.

[4] This month, just before the Passover month of Abib/Nisan, is usually equated with Feb./March. 1 Esdras 7:5 has the 23rd day, not the 3rd; but whether that was the true reading from which a word has dropped out in our text, or whether 1 Esdras has chosen a date which would allow a week's festivities to be immediately followed by the new year (*cf.* Brockington), remains uncertain.

## 6:16-18. The temple dedicated

The word for *dedication* (*ḥᵃnukkâ*) was later to become the name of a festival in memory of the Temple's re-consecration in 165 BC after its profanation by Antiochus Epiphanes (*cf*. Jn. 10:22f.). But it applied to anything newly made and put at God's disposal, from an altar to a person's house (Dt. 20:5) or a city wall (Ne. 12:27). Even the training of a child can be expressed in such language (Pr. 22:6, Heb.), though it would be unsafe to read too much into this.

The offerings were costly enough, yet incomparably outshone by the 22,000 oxen and 120,000 sheep (1 Ki. 8:63) of Solomon's dedication day. But the very contrast makes its own comment on that short-lived glory. This kingless, hard-pressed group was all that outwardly remained of it. The *sin offering for all Israel* was a more explicit comment; not on Solomon but on the nation as a whole. It was a confession of failure but also of faith. There was still atonement and still the covenant with the whole people—for this was the implication of the *twelve* sacrifices.

**18.** *The book of Moses* laid down the basic duties of priests and Levites, and the distinctions between them (*cf*., *e.g.*, Nu. 18); but the *divisions* and *courses* were the work of David: see on 2:36-39.

Note that this verse takes it for granted that the returned exiles had knowledge of the priestly law long before Ezra came to enforce it.

## 6:19-22. A joyful Passover

The feast followed only a few weeks after the dedication (see on verse 15). Rather appropriately the language of the story reverts now to Hebrew, only returning to Aramaic for the letter of Artaxerxes in 7:12-26. (The Aramaic section which has just ended had also begun with a letter in that language: 4:8ff.)

**21.** This is a crucial verse for correcting the impression one might gain from 4:1-3 of a bitterly exclusive party. That impression dies hard, but in reality we find that only the self-excluded were unwelcome. The convert found an open door, as Rahab and Ruth had done.

**22.** The word Assyria is a surprise here. If it is a copying error it is an early one, for it occurs in LXX. Perhaps, however, it is meant to awaken memories of the traditional oppressor (*cf*. Ne. 9:32), whose empire first Babylon and then Persia had inherited, but whose policies were now dramatically reversed.[1]

[1] The Persians themselves referred to this former province of Assyria as *Athura*

So ends the first stage, a generation long, of Israel's rehabilitation. It had opened when the Lord 'stirred up the spirit of Cyrus' (1 : 1), and it concluded with His turning the heart of one of that king's most powerful successors.

On this note of joy the narrative breaks off, to pass over in silence the long interval between the age of Zerubbabel and that of Ezra. The silence was punctuated in 4 : 6 by a single note from the reign of Xerxes (486–465/4). Elsewhere the book of Esther tells of distant events within that reign, centred on the royal city of Susa. At Jerusalem, Malachi may well have prophesied shortly before the coming of Ezra, giving us, if so, a sharp taste of the mood and temper of the times which occupy our chapters 7–10.

## Ezra 7 – 10

# THE PLUMB-LINE OF THE LAW

Now at last we meet the man from whom the whole book has taken its name. This chapter and the next will introduce the scholar-priest Ezra, his task and his expedition. The remaining two will show the moral disarray which he encountered at Jerusalem, and the unsparing counter-measures he applied. Much of the account is his personal record, using the 'I' and 'we' of direct speech.

### Ezra 7. Ezra's commission from Artaxerxes

#### 7:1-10. The man and his wisdom
These ten verses give an outline of the story which will be unfolded in detail and with many a personal touch in the rest of this chapter and chapter 8.

**1a.** The phrase, *Now after this*, puts nearly sixty years between this chapter and its precursor. Indeed some chronologies make the span considerably longer by identifying this *Artaxerxes* not with the first king of that name (464–423) but with the second (404–359), making Ezra's mission, in the seventh year (verse 7), take place not in 458 BC (as I hold) but in 398.[1]

---

(Assyria) in unofficial contexts (see A. F. Rainey *AJBA* I.2 (1969), pp. 51, 73 n.19).
[1] See Appendix IV, pp. 146–158.

**1b–5.** The genealogy vouches for Ezra as a priest (*cf.* 2:62); and the length at which it is given prepares us to meet a man of considerable importance.[1] His name stands very high in Jewish tradition, where he came to be regarded as a second Moses;[2] and indeed it was he, more than any other man, who stamped Israel with its lasting character as the people of a book.

**6.** With Ezra the picture of a scribe takes on more and more the features of a scholar and an expert in the sacred law. In his case it is emphasized by the word *skilled*, or literally 'rapid' (*cf.* Ps. 45:1 [2, Heb.])—suggesting a quickness of grasp and ease of movement amid this complex material which was the fruit of the devoted study described in verse 10. Incidentally the present verse shares none of the doubts of some modern criticism over the antiquity (*Moses*) or the authority (*the Lord*) of the law, nor does it see Ezra as a reviser or compiler. He is concerned with it as something *given*.

The last sentence of this verse supplies a detail which is absent from verses 11ff.: the fact that in God's prompting of the king, mentioned in verse 27, Ezra himself had a part to play (*all that he asked*). The courage it demanded can be gathered from Nehemiah's story of another such ordeal (Ne. 2:2ff.); but we are left in no doubt of the decisive factor: *the hand of the Lord*. That phrase becomes almost a refrain in these chapters (7:6, 9, 28; 8:18, 22, 31; Ne. 2:8, 18).

**7–10.** This little summary of the expedition gives no hint of the initial disappointment and delay, the fasting and prayer, and the dangers of such a journey, which will emerge in the full account. Here, however, we learn the length of time involved (four months, verse 9), and in verse 10 the secret of Ezra's lasting influence. He is a model reformer in that what he taught he had first lived, and what he lived he had first made sure of in the Scriptures. With study, conduct and teaching put deliberately in this right order, each of these was able to function properly at its best: study was saved from unreality, conduct from uncertainty, and teaching from insincerity and shallowness.

---

[1] Even so, it passes over several generations between Ezra and his ancestor Seraiah (1), who saw the fall of Jerusalem (2 Ki. 25:18) and whose son Jehozadak went into exile (1 Ch. 6:15). There are also seven names dropped apparently by an accident of copying, through the double occurrence of certain names in the family history (Amariah to Zadok, 1 Ch. 6:7f. and 11f.).

[2] For an extreme example see the apocryphal 2 Esdras 14, where Ezra is inspired to dictate to his assistants 94 books, consisting of apparently the entire OT plus 70 secret writings.

**7:11-26. Written authority for Ezra**

This letter, like the others in the book, is given in Aramaic (12-26), the language of official correspondence. It authorized Ezra, accompanied by any of his people who so wished (13), to go to Jerusalem to ensure the proper observance of the divine law (14, 25ff.). It also dealt with two matters of supply: first, a grant towards the cost of sacrifices (15-18), and an issue of Temple vessels (19); secondly, an order to the provincial treasurers, empowering Ezra to claim certain extra supplies (21-23), also exempting Temple officials of every grade from tax (24). Its final paragraph (25f.) called on Ezra to set up a judicial system with full powers of punishment, but also to see that people were not left in ignorance of the law.

A few points call for comment.

**12.** After *God of heaven*, the Aramaic adds the word *g<sup>e</sup>mîr*, 'perfect', which seems to have lost its companions. Probably the greeting, 'peace', should accompany it: *cf.*, *e.g.*, *'all* peace', 5:7.

**14.** *His seven counsellors*: cf. Esther 1:14.

**17.** The accurate knowledge of ritual requirements will have come from Ezra himself (note 'all that he asked', verse 6) or from a Jewish adviser at court. *Cf.* Nehemiah 11:24.

**19.** *The vessels* may have been some which had been overlooked when the captured vessels were restored by Cyrus (1:7ff.), but it is just as likely that they were a goodwill gift, newly presented.

**23.** *Lest his wrath be against the realm* ... is yet another expression of the concern that Cyrus had had (see on 1:2-4), and Darius after him (6:10), to win the goodwill of the gods worshipped in the empire. In more political terms (but religion and politics were inseparable), a prudent king would desire all possible contentment and good order among his subject people.

**24.** Darius had ordered a similar exemption for cult-servants of Apollo (see p. 19).

**25.** Notice the alternative description of the Torah as not only 'the law of your God' (14) but *'the wisdom* of your God'. It underlines the fact that Torah is a broader term than 'law', embracing instruction, indeed revelation, as well as commands.

*All the people in the province* must mean, in such a context, all to whom the Jewish law applies, whatever their distance from Jerusalem.[1]

---

[1] Ackroyd however insists on understanding an unqualified 'all', and ascribes

**26.** This power to inflict penalties, and *confiscation* in particular, was invoked in the divorce proceedings: see 10 : 8.

### 7:27, 28. A personal interjection[1]

We are suddenly aware of Ezra the man, his own voice breaking into the narrative with a grateful delight which time has done nothing to diminish. He will take up the history himself to the end of chapter 9; and Nehemiah, like him, will do most of his own narrating in the next book, sprinkling his story with even more vivid interjections and asides.

While verse 6, as we have seen, reveals that Ezra had to ask for all that he obtained, this doxology goes straight to what determined the issue: the inward work of God, who turns 'the king's heart . . . wherever he will' (Pr. 21 : 1). Verse 28, however, recalls the formidable array of courtiers which Ezra had had to brave, and the corresponding assurance that nothing less than *the hand of the Lord* was in this matter. On this expression see the final comment on verse 6. He would need this help just as much for the next task, for a powerful signature is sometimes easier to get, and to give, than the volunteers to take advantage of it.

### Ezra 8. Ezra's exodus

#### 8:1-14. The volunteers

**1.** Ezra knew the structure of his society well enough to direct his appeal to the *heads* of families (7 : 28; 8 : 1), knowing that in most cases if they came they would bring their groups with them. See verses 3-14 for the effect of this policy.[2]

Note the words *with me*, in the opening sentence (which GNB gratuitously alters to 'with Ezra'). It is personal reporting, continuing from 7 : 27f. to the end of chapter 9, apart from a brief return to the third person in 8 : 35f., where 'they' takes over from 'we' for two verses.

---

it to the writer's idealized vision of the province as brought entirely under Jewish rule. But most commentators credit the biblical writer and his readers with more realism than this.

[1] From this point onward, the language is Heb. (The Aramaic sections were 4 : 8 - 6 : 18, and 7 : 12-26.)

[2] It is at least food for thought that church strategy often tends to reverse this order, concentrating on the children, the tail-end of the family, to the neglect of the head.

**2-14.** The interest of this forbidding list of names and numbers lies in the fact that in every case but one these groups are joining, at long last, the descendants of the pioneers from their own family stock, who had been in the first party to return from Babylon eighty years before. The family names in verses 4-14 can all (except Joab, verse 9) be found in 2 : 3-15,[1] and the present list opens with two priests (evidently accompanied by several of their relatives: see on verse 24) and a descendant of David (2), who have likewise been preceded by their kinsmen. So it underlines the fact that the original challenge to return, in the days of Cyrus, had had a very mixed response, dividing individual clans down the middle—though Zechariah 6 : 9-11 and the book of Esther illustrate the strong fellow-feeling that could still bind them together. There is nothing to indicate that even now these families were complete, leaving none of their members behind.[2]

## 8 : 15-20. The missing Levites

The three-day pause by the river[3] was no waste of time: this was the right moment to take stock and be prepared for unwelcome discoveries. The absence of Levites and other Temple servants is a revealing contretemps; it was only natural for these men to shrink from a prospect which was doubly daunting: not only the uprooting which all the pilgrims faced, but the drastic change from ordinary pursuits to the strict routines of the Temple. So it is no surprise to read of Ezra's careful choice of emissaries to rectify this (nine of them for the weight they carried in the community, and an extra two for their diplomatic skill, verse 16), and to notice his explicit briefing of them ('telling them what to say' and whom to approach, 17).[4]

---

[1] As RSV mg. shows, Zattu (5) and Bani (10) are found not in the Heb. text but in the corresponding list in 1 Esdras 8 : 32, 36. The pattern of the neighbouring verses confirms the probability that 1 Esdras has rightly preserved, rather than added, these names.

[2] Possibly verse 13 should be translated 'the last (of the family)', as Brockington suggests; but 'those who came later' (RSV, *etc.*) seems more likely.

[3] The expression, 'the river that runs (lit. comes) to Ahava', suggests a canal, since it is named after its destination (*cf.* verse 31, 'the Ahava canal'?). There were many canals in Babylonia. The location of Ahava is unknown.

[4] The choice of Casiphia (its location is unknown as yet) suggests that there was a sanctuary there, and this may also be indicated by the repeated expression 'the place' (17), which was sometimes a synonym for a holy place (*cf.* Dt. 12 : 2, 3, 5). We know of a Jewish temple at Elephantine, on the Nile, at this period.

**18.** The outcome was highly satisfying, not only numerically but in the provision of a gifted leader; and Ezra, as ever, recognized in this *the good hand of our God upon us*. On this phrase, see on 7:6.

**20.** On *the temple servants*, or Nethinim, see on 2:43-54, where they are discussed at some length.

## 8:21-23. To seek ... a straight way
Ezra's heart-searching and his candour about it bring him very close to the Christian who has wrestled with this kind of issue on a smaller scale. And there is an added interest in the fact that Nehemiah, in his day, would see the matter quite differently, accepting a military escort as part of God's bounty (Ne. 2:7-9). Both were attitudes of faith, and each in its different way (like the options in Rom. 14:6) gave acceptable honour to God.

## 8:24-30. The priests as treasurers
It now emerges that the two heads of priestly families who were mentioned in verse 2 must have brought with them a number of their kinsmen, as did the other chief men in that company (*cf.* 3-14).[1] The treasure now entrusted to them for the journey was enormous (a *talent* weighed about 30 kilograms). Ezra's refusal to have an armed guard, and his reminder to the priests of their sacred trust (28), gave them an abrupt initiation into the discipline of faith.

Artaxerxes, like his predecessors, marked the occasion by an official gift, and called on Jews who were not joining the expedition to add their share (25). It was a corollary of his authorization of the enterprise. If the God of the Jews were no more than a name (he might have argued), the whole exercise was pointless; but if He existed, He would expect tangible courtesies from a king—and the scale of them should reflect the donor's power and majesty.

## 8:31-34. The journey and arrival
**31.** *The twelfth day* is consistent with 'the first day' in 7:9,

[1] Verse 24 reads as though Sherebiah and his companions were priests, whereas verses 18f. and Ne. 12:24ff. show that they were only Levites. Probably NEB is right in following the reading in 1 Esdras 8:54 where the word 'and' precedes the name Sherebiah. *I.e.*, as verse 30 confirms, the treasure was entrusted to priests *and* Levites, *viz.*, 'twelve of the chiefs of the priests, together with Sherebiah', *etc.* (verse 24, NEB).

when Ezra 'began to go up . . .'; in fact the events of 8:15-23 were pushed through with remarkable speed.

The word for *ambushes* is singular here, *i.e.*, collective, and the sentence is better rendered 'and he saved us from enemy attack and from ambush on the way' (NEB)—implying probably an absence of such events rather than a series of escapes.

**32.** The journey of nearly a thousand miles is passed over with scarcely a comment. All that mattered was the destination and the mission to fulfil.

**33, 34.** The procedure was businesslike, and the implication is that nothing was missing, despite the immense and hazardous journey. Such was 'the hand of our God . . . upon us' (31).

Some of these names will meet us again in the book of Nehemiah: *viz.*, Meremoth (Ne. 3:4, 21), Jozabad (Ne. 11:16) and Binnui (Ne. 3:24).

### 8:35, 36. Obligations to fulfil

These two verses (using the third person) add a few details to supplement Ezra's own account, which will continue in chapter 9.

**35.** Homage and dedication were the keynotes of the burnt offering, and atonement the emphasis of the sin offering. The number *twelve* and its multiple, *ninety-six*, signified *all Israel*. The reason for offering *seventy-seven* lambs is not so obvious, whatever conjectures about the perfect number it may seem to invite. Possibly 1 Esdras 8:66 is right with 'seventy-two', another multiple of twelve.

**36.** After the Godward obligations come those that were manward. *The king's commissions* were presumably the documents that accredited Ezra as one who was authorized to administer the Jewish law among his fellow-countrymen in the various regions of the province. This wider authority, extending beyond the immediate area round Jerusalem, was mentioned in 7:25f.

The final sentence should correct any impression that Ezra's mission was purely disciplinary. His intention was constructive, and the situation revealed in the next chapter, which demanded painful measures, clearly took him by surprise.

### Ezra 9. The scandal of mixed marriages

### 9:1-5. Ezra is told the news

**1, 2.** There is a strong flavour of the books of Moses in the way the mixed marriages were reported to Ezra. The list of foreign peoples in verse 1, with its archaic sound, recalls at once the string of names which, with minor variants, had been a keynote of the ancient promises and warnings about Canaan.[1] In particular, there is a pointed resemblance to Exodus 34:11-16 and Deuteronomy 7:1-4, where lists that are markedly similar to this introduce the ban on foreign marriages.

So Ezra's campaign to spread the knowledge of Scripture was bearing the characteristic fruit of reform less than five months after his arrival (*cf.* 7:9 with 10:9). It had thrown new light not only on a tolerated evil but on the high calling of this community as a *holy race*[2] (2) and as heirs of the Exodus (re-enacted, in a new form, in their own time: *cf.* Is. 48:20f.). And with no prompting from Ezra this had dawned on the group of leaders who now approached him with a report that was news to him. It is also remarkable that these men, *the officials* (*śārîm*, the usual term for the chief men of the nation), were evidently the established leaders, who had hitherto accepted the anomalies. It was not an initiative by the newcomers, who would have had less temptation to hush the matter up.

**3-5.** Ezra's reaction was typical of him. It was almost inaction, yet more potent than any flurry of activity, since it drew out of other people the initiatives that could best come from them. The successive verbs that concern him in this episode are nearly all of this kind: verbs of distress and abasement and of intercession. Matthew Henry, commenting on Nehemiah 13:25, drew a neat contrast between Ezra and his more militant successor: Nehemiah plucking out the offenders' hair, Ezra plucking out his own. For another comparison between them, see on 8:21-23, above.

### 9:6-15. Ezra's prayer

Something of the devotion and insight of the man praying can be sensed in this confession. His involvement with those for whom he spoke comes through at once, in the swift transition from 'I', in the first sentence, to 'our' and 'we' for the rest of the prayer. Ezra could have protested his innocence, but like the servant in Isaiah 53:12 he was impelled to reckon himself 'numbered with the

---

[1] Gn. 15:19-21; Ex. 3:8, 17; 13:5; 23:23; 33:2; 34:11; *etc.*
[2] Lit. 'the holy seed': *cf.*, in various terms, Gn. 28:14; Ex. 19:6; Mal. 2:15. The Heb. expression, 'the holy seed', occurs in Is. 6:13.

transgressors', more deeply *ashamed* of the national *guilt* than any of them[1], and thus more fit to be their spokesman in confession. Secondly, he could not forget the havoc they had suffered—and deserved (7)—especially in their loss of freedom (note the words *captivity* (7), *bondage* (8, 9), *bondmen* (9), and the decimation of their numbers, stressed in the recurrence of the word *remnant*: 8, 13, 14, 15). In other words, he had a high sense of the glory they had betrayed, and he could not be reconciled to what they had become. But thirdly, he was acutely conscious of God's mercy. The very fact that any remnant had survived was proof of it (8), for even their punishment had been mercifully light (13), and verses 8 and 9 use vivid terms—characteristically concrete[2]—for God's many-sided loving-kindness. At the same time, it was a mere shadow of what God could do and give—*a little reviving* (8), *some reviving* (9)—and it was in jeopardy already, after this *brief moment* (8) of grace; for even the eighty years since Cyrus were no more than that in God's perspective.

From verse 10 the confession becomes specific, allowing the word of God to frame its own indictment. Verses 11 and 12 give the substance of such a passage as Deuteronomy 7:1-3, but the mention of *the prophets* (plural; *i.e.*, not Moses only) suggests that the message had also been preached. There is a sample of such preaching, by a probable contemporary, in Malachi 2:10-16.

The prayer ends with clear recognition that God has every reason to wash His hands of this community, as He had once threatened to do with an earlier generation (Ex. 32:10). This was no exaggerated fancy. There were other Israelites scattered abroad, through whom the promises could be fulfilled. Ezra had not even the heart to plead, as Moses had, that God's name would suffer in such a case. His prayer was naked confession, without excuses, without the pressure of so much as a request.

### Ezra 10. The severing of ties

### 10:1-8. The people's initiative
Instead of whipping a reluctant people into action, Ezra has

---

[1] *Cf.* Je. 6:15, spoken of an earlier generation: 'No, they were not at all ashamed; they did not know how to blush.'

[2] The *secure hold* (8) is lit. a nail, stake or tent-peg (*cf.* Is. 22:23; 54:2), and the *protection* (9) is lit. a wall. Like the former, the latter, as Ackroyd points out, is 'clearly metaphorical' (as in Ps. 80:12) and not to be confused with the city wall (for which a different word is used) rebuilt by Nehemiah.

pricked their conscience to the point at which they now urge *him* to act. His apparent despair provokes them to seek *hope for Israel* at any cost (2f.), and his abandonment to grief stirs them to impatience for some more positive response—witness in verse 4 their brisk advice and earnest pledge of help. So the extreme measures which he now made every section of society accept on oath (5) were wholly of their choosing, and all the more binding for that. Even his advice played only a modest part: *the counsel of my lord*[1] took its place within the consensus of the godly and the prescriptions of the law (3). As far as we can see, that counsel was not even explicit; only an inference from his dismay.

**6.** Ezra's resort to more assertive acts, in verse 5, was strictly limited. The words, 'Then Ezra arose' (5), give way as soon as possible to the sequel, *Then Ezra withdrew*; and the withdrawal was to solitary fasting and mourning. This privacy confirms, incidentally, the evidence from his public prayers, in Ezra 9 and Nehemiah 9, that his dramatic gestures of dismay were utterly sincere. They had a powerful impact, but were not contrivances: they came from the heart. Nor were they escapist: they left room for other men's response but, given that response, Ezra spoke and acted with decision (5, 10f.).

On the suggested relevance of *Jehohanan* to the date of Ezra's mission, see Appendix IV, pp. 153-155.

**7, 8.** The *proclamation* was a corporate one (lit. 'they issued a proclamation'), not put out in Ezra's name alone, although he had the emperor's authority to punish (7:26). What would carry more moral weight than imperial decrees was the order (or 'counsel',[2] as in verse 3) of the local leaders. The word *forfeited* is very strong: it is mostly used of the destruction ordered against special enemies, *e.g.*, Jericho, but it could have the weaker sense of 'confiscated' for priestly use: *cf.* Leviticus 27:21.

### 10:9-15. The mass meeting at Jerusalem

It was late in the year, well into the equivalent of December, and

[1] The Massoretes read this word as *'aḏōnāy*, *i.e.*, 'the Lord' (God); but apart from Vulg., the ancient and modern versions (and 1 Esdras) agree in taking it as *'aḏōnî*, 'my lord'. The consonants are the same, and while either alternative is possible, the latter seems preferable in view of the stronger terms used in the rest of the verse for what God Himself says.

[2] NEB translates this: 'it should be within the discretion of the chief officers . . . to confiscate', *etc.* This is possible, but the run of the sentence seems to favour the more usual translation. Presumably the court's power of discretion in hard cases hardly needed stating.

verse 9 captures for us the shivering misery of the scene. Ezra is characteristically absorbed with the main issue (10f.), but no less typically he is open to reason and the initiatives of others. In this vivid little paragraph we can picture the build-up of suggestions as the crowd takes over the talking and makes its various points—not without some contrary voices. Of the dissentients in verse 15, *Meshullam* may have been one of the 'leading men' in the group which returned with Ezra (*cf.* 8 : 16), and *Shabbethai*, as a Levite, would have counted as one who had more than a layman's knowledge of the law. There is no comment on their opposition, which could have been motivated by a variety of reasons, not necessarily dishonourable. None of their names appears in the list of interested parties in verses 18–44 except Meshullam's (15, 29); but his was an extremely common name at the time.[1] There may have been friends or relatives whom some of these four men wished to shelter; on the other hand the harshness of the remedy and the lack of any obvious legal requirement of it could have stirred the same misgivings in them as in a modern reader.

One fact to be borne in mind about the issue as a whole is that divorce was permitted in Israel, though not without some serious cause (Dt. 24 : 1); and broken marriages had been rife at this time for the very opposite of the present reason: *i.e.*, there had been a scandalous number of Jewish wives abandoned in favour of heathen women (Mal. 2 : 10–16). While divorce is always hateful to God (Mal. 2 : 16), and a witness to human 'hardness of heart' (Mk. 10 : 5), the situation described in Ezra 9 and 10 was a classic example of one in which the lesser of two evils had to be chosen. If a serious reason for divorce could ever exist, this had a better claim than most to come within that category.

Presumably because divorce was nothing new in Israel, except on this appalling scale, we are not told what was done for these victims of it. It seems most likely that in such a case a wife would return to her own family; but this is no more than an assumption. We simply lack the knowledge of what was customary.

## 10:16–44. The legal proceedings

The fact that the hearings took three months proved the wisdom of having second thoughts about settling everything in a day or

---

[1] There are at least ten different Meshullams mentioned in Ezra-Nehemiah, two of them in almost contiguous verses, Ne. 3 : 4, 6.

two and in a crowd (*cf.* 12-14). But it also showed how far the trouble had spread. Clearly Ezra had not foreseen a task of this size.

**18.** Where we might have expected some cover-up of priestly guilt, this catalogue goes out of its way to give it prominence, with true biblical candour, by reversing the order followed in chapter 2. There it was the lay Israelites who were enumerated first; here it is their spiritual leaders, headed by descendants of the honoured high priest Jeshua-ben-Jozadak (*cf.* 3:2; 5:2, *etc.*). Clearly neither ancestry nor office can be a guarantee of moral probity. It may even be significant that the priests, who made up 10 per cent of the company in chapter 2, supply 15 per cent of the cases here.[1]

**19.** Although the pledge and guilt offering are mentioned only at this point, they are probably to be taken as the standard procedure throughout the list. *They pledged themselves* is literally 'they gave their hands': as common a way of clinching an agreement as our handshake (*cf.* 2 Ki. 10:15; Ezk. 17:18). On the offering for guilt, note verse 10; see also, *e.g.*, Leviticus 5:17-19, where the point is made that even unwitting breaches of God's law create guilt and require atonement.

**23, 24.** The Levites and these two subdivisions of them are grouped in the same way in 2:40-42.

**25ff.** Nine of the thirty-three families and town groups which appeared in 2:3-35 are represented here, and there are two new ones: a second Bani family (34) and that of Binnui (38).

**44.** As the margin indicates, the last half of this verse is obscure,[2] and most modern versions rely on the parallel in 1 Esdras 9:36, which not only makes sense but is informative, showing that the policy advocated in verse 3 was adopted.

On this painful note the story of Ezra's ministry breaks off. It is appropriate enough. His mission was to apply the law to his people (7:14), and the law brings the knowledge of sin. But a postscript will follow, when Ezra will present the positive and festive aspects of the law: its gift of light to the mind (Ne. 8:8), and its witness to God as liberator and provider (Ne. 8:9-18).

---

[1] Too much weight must not be put on this, since the ratio of priests to the community could well have changed in these 80 years. But at least the priests seem to have been no better than their fellows.

[2] Lit. the Heb. says: 'and some of them (masc.) were women, and they (masc.) appointed sons.' Such a tangle is proof of a damaged text, to make sense of which involves more violence than to accept the alternative version.

Until that moment, some thirteen years beyond the events of this chapter, Ezra will disappear from the record. Meanwhile further trials will overtake the Jewish settlers, until Nehemiah arrives to transform the scene.

In the Hebrew Bible the book of Nehemiah follows straight on from here, to form the final part of a single story.

NEHEMIAH

# NEHEMIAH

More than half this book is a personal record, punctuated with 'asides' and frank comments which make it (in such parts) one of the liveliest pieces of writing in the Bible. Much of Ezra's story was also told in the first person (Ezr. 8 : 15 – 9 : 15), but Ezra was a quieter personality than the formidable, practical Nehemiah; he does not leap out of the page as this man does.

The main action is crowded into the spring and summer of the year 445 BC, in which time Nehemiah not only made the journey from near the Persian Gulf to Jerusalem, but restored the city's walls and gates, and began to see to its defence. All this he recounts himself.

From chapter 8, to near the end of chapter 12, another voice takes up the story, to tell of the spiritual fortifying of the same community, by the reading of the law, an act of penitence and a special covenant, and by provision for the worship that God required.

Then (12 : 31ff.) Nehemiah himself depicts for us the dedication day, with its twin processions and its loud rejoicings for the restoration of the city walls. Finally, in chapter 13, he leaves us with some vigorous reminders that a running battle is still in progress. Clearly his twelve years as governor, and his temporary return to the imperial court, have done nothing to slow down his reactions or to cool his fighting spirit. If Judaism was to earn a name for its zeal for righteousness, it owed it very largely to these two determined men, Ezra and Nehemiah.

## Nehemiah 1. Sad news from home

### 1:1-3. The plight of Jerusalem

**1.** In our terms the date of this conversation, which set in motion the great events of this book, was between mid-November and mid-December, 446 BC, and the approach to the king in chapter 2 will have taken place in the following March/April, 445. Both are reckoned here to fall within the twentieth year[1] of Artaxerxes, who reigned from 464 to 423. It

---

[1] By our calendar, the Persian calendar, and the normal Jewish calendar which starts with Nisan (2 : 1), *i.e.*, March/April, the date in 1 : 1 would have to fall in the king's 19th year, since the 20th year is corroborated elsewhere for the

was about thirteen years since Ezra had set out for Jerusalem (Ezr. 7:7).[1]

*Susa the capital (bîrâ)*, or better, 'Susa, the citadel' (*cf.* Est. 3:15, where it is perhaps distinct from the general 'city of Susa'), was the winter resort of the Persian kings.

**2.** Hanani may have been a brother or no more than a kinsman, since one word serves for both. He reappears in 7:2 as a man whom Nehemiah could entrust with high office. In the question and answer, the word *escaped* is akin to one of Isaiah's favourite expressions, 'the remnant'—that little portion of Israel with whom the future was to lie. In fact Nehemiah's choice of words, echoed by his brother, may have been a conscious allusion to the promise of a 'remnant' and 'survivors', who would not merely escape destruction but 'lean upon the Lord … in truth' (Is. 10:20-22).

**3.** The reply would be badly misunderstood if we just took it to speak of the ruins left by Nebuchadrezzar. That was ancient history (587 BC), but this was news and a shattering blow. Its most likely background is the sequence in Ezra 4:7-23, in which a bid to rebuild the walls had been reported to king Artaxerxes and promptly crushed 'by force and power'. It was an ominous development, for the ring of hostile neighbours round Jerusalem could now claim royal backing. The patronage which Ezra had enjoyed (*cf.* Ezr. 7:21-26) was suddenly in ruins, as completely as the city walls and gates. Jerusalem was not only disarmed but on its own.

### 1:4-11. The prayer of Nehemiah

**4.** Since Nehemiah's natural bent was for swift, decisive action, his behaviour here is remarkable. It shows where his priorities lay. It also reveals, by every phrase in this verse, the

---

events of 2:1ff. (*cf.* 5:14). But there are indications that the OT adopted for some of its datings of kings an autumn-to-autumn reckoning: *cf.* E. R. Thiele, *The Mysterious Numbers of the Hebrew Kings* (Chicago, 1951; Paternoster, 1966), p. 30; see, however, D. J. A. Clines, *JBL* 93 (1974), pp. 25, 34-36. An alternative explanation is that 'twentieth' in 1:1 is an editorial or scribal error. The omission of the king's name may indicate some textual abnormality in the verse. This seems to involve fewer difficulties than the autumn-to-autumn hypothesis, since the other dates in Ne. are based on the normal calendar which started the year with the Passover month Nisan (formerly known as Abib) and held the feast of Tabernacles in the 7th month (Lv. 23:34; Ne. 8:2, 14).

[1] On this disputed point, see Appendix IV, pp. 146-158.

unhurried and far from superficial background to the famous 'arrow prayer' of 2:4 and to the achievements which were to follow it.

**5.** There is more than rhetoric in this elaborate opening. It deliberately postpones the cry for help, which could otherwise be faithless and self-pitying. It mounts immediately to *heaven* (as the Lord's prayer does), where the perspective will be right, and it reflects on the character of God—not only for its encouraging aspect of staunchness and love, but first of all for the majesty which puts man, whether friend or foe, in his place.

**6, 7.** The remembrance of God's covenant, in verse 5, has raised the matter of the partner's response (to 'love him and keep his commandments', 5c). This inevitably leads to heart-searching and confession, in which Nehemiah, faced with such a standard, owns to personal (6c) as well as corporate guilt. He will have to come empty-handed with his requests.

**8-10.** He is empty-handed, but not uninvited. He knows the threats and promises of Scripture well enough to make a strong, not a tentative plea. He draws on several passages of Deuteronomy (*cf.* verse 8b with Dt. 28:64; verse 9 with Dt. 30:1-4 and Dt. 12:5). Most significantly in verse 10 he quotes the words in which Moses had pleaded for Israel on mount Sinai (Dt. 9:29), that God would stand by His own (*thy servants and thy people*) and by the work He had so strenuously begun. At that point Israel had been threatened with extinction; now, it seems, Nehemiah sees the situation as hardly less perilous. Like Moses, he must stand in the breach[1] with his intercession.

**11.** The prayer comes to a sudden point with the words *today* and *this man*. It has been no substitute for action. And Nehemiah has kept a surprise in store for the reader, who has so far had no inkling of his position or the identity of 'this man'.

The *cupbearer* (the same word as the 'butler' of the Joseph story, Gn. 40:2ff.) was a high official in the royal household, whose basic duty of choosing and tasting the wine to demonstrate that it was not poisoned, and of presenting it to the king, gave him frequent access to the king's presence and made him potentially a man of influence. Myers draws attention to a statement of Herodotus on the honour in which the Persians held this office, and to the portrayal in Tobit 1:22 of Ahikar as not only the

---

[1] *Cf.* Ps. 106:23.

cupbearer but the chief minister of the Assyrian king Esarhaddon.[1]

## Nehemiah 2. The author is sent to Jerusalem

### 2:1-8. The matter is broached

**1, 2.** The mention of the month *Nisan*, roughly the equivalent of April and the beginning of the Persian and Jewish year, reveals how long Nehemiah had persisted in fasting and prayer (*cf.* 1 : 4). It was four months since the news had reached him. Now his praying had reached the point recorded in 1 : 11, the time for action.

Perhaps, as many have suggested, his alarm at the king's comment on his dejection sprang from sudden awareness of a breach of etiquette—for a servant's private feelings are usually best kept to himself, especially if they will strike a jarring note. But while this makes good sense, the reason surely lies deeper. Nehemiah has resolved to speak out 'today' (1 : 11). He may even have decided to precipitate the enquiry by allowing his feelings to be obvious. Now the moment has come, and if he mishandles it there will not be another. Further, he will be asking the king to revise his policy, for the decision against Jerusalem had been official. True, the decree had left a loophole for change (see on Ezr. 4 : 21), but so quick a *volte-face* would be a great deal to ask of anyone; and 'a king's wrath is a messenger of death.'[2]

**3.** The subject is sensitively introduced. One can make perhaps too much of the fact that, as Myers points out, Jerusalem is not named anywhere in this conversation—for it is clearly implied by verse 8. But certainly Nehemiah, like Esther,[3] had the wisdom to present the matter first as news of a personal blow, not as a political issue. At whatever stage in the conversation *the city, the place of my fathers' sepulchres*, was revealed to be Jerusalem, the king's sympathy had been already enlisted, and his readiness to help already made clear (4).

**4, 5.** The remembered scene lives for us in this intimate, rapid narrative. We are involved in it, holding our breath with

---

[1] One version of the LXX (B) makes Nehemiah a 'eunuch' (*eunouchos*) instead of a 'cupbearer' (*oinochoos*); but this has no basis in the Heb. text, and has the marks of a confusion between the two similar Greek words. (On the conjecture that the Persian title Tirshatha should be translated 'eunuch', see footnote on Ezr. 2 : 63.)
[2] Pr. 16 : 14.
[3] Est. 8 : 3f.

Nehemiah as he gasps a prayer and braces himself to reply. The exchanges are characteristic: the suppliant speaks with the slight verbosity that courtesy demands; the king with the brevity of one whose habitual role is to decide matters. Each of his questions goes straight to the next point.

**6.** The mention of *the queen* may indicate that this was a private occasion, since apparently it was not customary for the queen to appear at a formal banquet. It also may suggest that the king's decision owed something to her influence. The whole interview gives the impression that it was Nehemiah's personal qualities that won him the right to speak and that gained his point, overriding all the political obstacles.

The *time* set for his return will hardly have been the twelve years mentioned in 5:14 and 13:6. He is more likely to have reported back after the dedication of the walls, within the year, and then to have had his appointment as governor renewed.

**7, 8.** If we are impressed with the realism and boldness of these requests, so too was the king. Vagueness, at this point, would have shown up the project as a mere dream or sudden impulse; but Nehemiah had prayed long enough (see on verse 1), and had had faith enough, to visualize the operation in some detail, even to the building technique he would be using for the wall (on which, see on Ezr. 5:8). But the decisive factor, as he recognized, was not his faith but the object of it: the God who was his God, whose *good (i.e.,* gracious) *hand* was upon him. *Cf.* verse 18 and the references at Ezra 7:6.

## 2:9-16. The journey, arrival and night survey

**9.** There was more than protection to be gained from the military escort. It meant an arrival in style, impressively reinforcing the presentation of credentials to the neighbouring governors, and making very plain the change of royal policy (see on 1:3; 2:2). It may help to explain why Nehemiah's enemies resorted to bluff instead of force in their campaign against him. On Ezra's disdain for an armed escort, see the comment on Ezra 8:21-23. (On *the province Beyond the River*, see on Ezr. 4:10 and 5:3.)

**10.** These two men will throw a long shadow over the story. Both of them were men of influence and power, as can be seen not only from the connections they established with the high priest's family (13:4ff., 28), but from outside sources as well. A document of 407 BC (38 years after the events of this chapter) refers to Sanballat as 'governor of Samaria',[1] and the Jewish name *Tobiah* is borne by a powerful family in Ammon for centuries to come. There is little doubt that the label, *the servant*, or 'slave' (NEB), was a contemptuous abbreviation of a title, 'the king's servant', and that *the Ammonite* described not Tobiah's ancestry but his chosen sphere, in which he had gained high office.[2]

**11-15.** Nehemiah, as ever, is a model of good sense, piety and attention to detail. For all his speed and drive, he does not rush into action (11) or into talk (12). He anticipates the obvious objection that a newcomer can have no idea of the task, so he briefs himself thoroughly and chooses his moment to show his hand (16). He has not only kept his plans from the enemy: he has kept the initiative *vis-à-vis* the leaders whom he must convince and arouse. He would have lost this if he had been exposing half-formed ideas piecemeal to every acquaintance. Above and beyond his sound tactics, however, was the conviction that basically the project was not his. It was from God and 'for Jerusalem' (12)—not from Nehemiah nor for his prestige.

The route that he followed in his night survey can only be reconstructed by conjecture, at this distance in time. Of the names in this passage, we know from 3:13 that the *Valley Gate* (mentioned also in 2 Ch. 26:9) and the *Dung Gate* were about 500 yards apart; it is also fairly certain that the Dung Gate was at the city's southern or south-eastern extremity, leading to the refuse-tip, the Valley of Hinnom (Gehenna). It may have been an alternative name for the Potsherd (*i.e.*, rubbish) Gate of Jeremiah 19:2. The *Fountain Gate* evidently led to the spring

---

[1] See the Elephantine papyri in, *e.g.*, *ANET*, p. 492b; *DOTT*, p. 264. He may not have reached this status by the time Nehemiah crossed his path, since verse 10 speaks of his hearing the news, not of his receiving the credentials of verse 9. The papyri imply that by 407 he was an old man, his power delegated to his sons. This ties in with his being the Sanballat who was Nehemiah's contemporary.

[2] Tobiah ('Yahweh is good') is a Jewish name, not an Ammonite one. Evidence of this family's long-continued prominence in Ammon is found in an inscription at 'Araq el-Emir, and again in a letter of 259 BC among the Zenon papyri which shows a Tobiah (Tubias) in office under Ptolemy II. At Jerusalem in the 2nd century BC the Tobiads were to have a corrupting influence on religion and politics in the period that led up to the persecution by Antiochus Epiphanes. Some have seen the beginning of all these events in the partial rejection of 'the sons of Tobiah' in Ezr. 2:59f. for their lack of an attested pedigree. Enmity and defection could well have been the reaction to such a rebuff, but there is no means of proving that the Tobiahs in Ammon were members of this family. For archaeological and literary details see C. C. McCown, 'The 'Araq el-Emir and the Tobiads', *BA* 20 (1957), pp. 63-76.

called En Rogel near the south-eastern corner, where the Hinnom and Kidron valleys meet, since another gate further up the eastern side (the Water Gate, 3:26) gave access to the other main spring, the Gihon. Opinions differ over the *King's Pool*, but the reference in 3:15 to 'the Pool of Shelah of the king's garden' seems to support K. M. Kenyon's identification of it with Hezekiah's Pool of Siloam 'lying beside the [southern] tip of the eastern ridge'.[1] The name Shelah (*šelaḥ*, 3:15) is closely related to *šilôaḥ*, the Hebrew equivalent of the word Siloam, and comes from the root 'to send', *i.e.*, to bring in water by a conduit.

It seems, then, that Nehemiah set out from the west side of the city, coming out of the ruined gateway and turning left towards the south, and so round to the eastern side. There he was soon forced to dismount and proceed on foot along this ridge above the Kidron valley (14b, 15a), before turning back[2] and re-entering the city at his starting-point. The obstruction may well have been the huge spill of rubble, evidently from Nebuchadnezzar's assault, which was re-discovered in Dr Kathleen Kenyon's 1961-3 excavations.[3]

**2:17-20. Reactions to the plan**

Sometimes it takes a stranger to see sharply what has been softened by familiarity. Nehemiah's perspective is significant. On the debit side it is the *disgrace*, not the insecurity of their position, which strikes him—for Jerusalem should be seen as 'the city of the great King' and 'the joy of all the earth'.[4] And on the credit side he speaks first of *the hand of . . . God* upon him, and only then of *the words (of) the king*. This was indeed the right order, as cause and effect. It was also his genuine conviction—see the end of verse 8—and as such it was infectious. But in truth, so total a response from such a group was as miraculous as that of Artaxerxes.

**19.** A third name is now added to those of Sanballat and Tobiah. There is evidence that *Geshem* (*cf.* 6:1ff.), far from being a negligible alien, was an even more powerful figure than his companions, though probably less earnestly committed to their

---

[1] K. M. Kenyon, *Digging up Jerusalem* (Ernest Benn, 1974), p. 181.
[2] Brockington however points out that 'I turned back and entered' could be a common Hebraism for 'I re-entered', and does not exclude the possibility that the circuit was completed.
[3] See *BA* 27 (1964), pp. 34-52, esp. p. 45.
[4] Ps. 48:2.

cause. His name appears on a silver vessel donated to an Arabian goddess Han-'ilat towards the end of the 5th century BC, *i.e.*, within approximately the next forty years after these events. The inscription names the donor as 'Cain (Qaynu) son of Geshem (Gashmu), king of Qedar'.[1] From other sources it emerges that Geshem and his son ruled a league of Arabian tribes which took control of Moab and Edom (Judah's neighbours to the east and south) together with part of Arabia and the approaches to Egypt, under the Persian empire.

So, with already a hostile Samaria and Ammon to the north and east, Judah was now virtually encircled, and the war of nerves had begun. There was an edge to the taunts in the word *rebelling*, for a case could always be trumped up which might change the king's mind and excuse an attack or an assassination.

**20.** Even to his enemies Nehemiah produces as his trump card not his mandate from the king but his authority from God. There is, too, a fine ring of pride in his citizenship, however down-at-heel Jerusalem at this moment might appear. In the three words, *portion . . . right . . . memorial*, he dismisses the past, present and future of these unenviable outsiders. The positive aspect of so spirited an attitude is well caught in John Newton's lines on Psalm 87:

> Saviour, since of Zion's city
>     I through grace a member am,
> Let the world deride or pity,
>     I will glory in Thy name:
> Fading is the worldling's pleasure,
>     All his boasted pomp and show;
> Solid joys and lasting treasure
>     None but Zion's children know.

## Nehemiah 3. The work is shared out

This catalogue of largely forgotten names and places reveals an extraordinary feat of organization and concerted action. It has all the marks of a shared enthusiasm, shown in the heterogeneous groups which set to work on their adjacent stretches of wall, some as family units, others by towns, crafts (*e.g.*, the goldsmiths, and the perfumer of verse 8), trades (the merchants: 31f.) and callings

[1] See F. M. Cross, Jr., 'Geshem the Arabian, Enemy of Nehemiah', in *BA* 18 (1955), pp. 46f. On the form Gashmu see Ne. 6:6, mg.

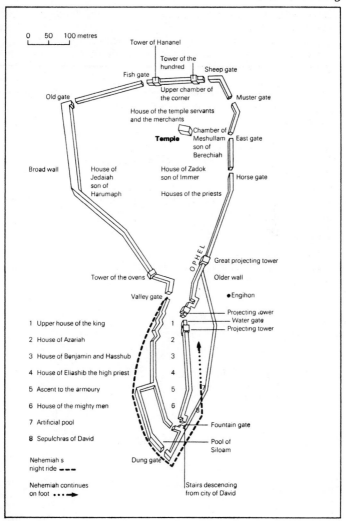

0  50  100 metres

Tower of Hananel

Tower of the hundred

Sheep gate

Fish gate

Old gate

Muster gate

Upper chamber of the corner

House of the temple servants and the merchants

Chamber of Meshullam son of Berechiah

**Temple**

East gate

Broad wall

House of Jedaiah son of Harumaph

House of Zadok son of Immer

Horse gate

Houses of the priests

OPHEL

Great projecting tower

Older wall

Tower of the ovens

•Engihon

Valley gate

Projecting tower
Water gate
Projecting tower

1  Upper house of the king

2  House of Azariah

3  House of Benjamin and Hasshub

4  House of Eliashib the high priest

5  Ascent to the armoury

6  House of the mighty men

7  Artificial pool

8  Sepulchres of David

Nehemiah s night ride ▬ ▬ ▬

Nehemiah continues on foot • • •➤

Fountain gate

Pool of Siloam

Dung gate

Stairs descending from city of David

Nehemiah's Jerusalem (after Aharoni and Avi-Yonah). The site names are derived from Ne. 3:1–32, proceeding anti-clockwise from the Sheep Gate at the NE corner.

85

(the priests: 1, 21f., 28; Levites: 17f.; temple servants: 26; district officers: 9, 12, 15-17). One man has even mobilized his daughters (12; see comment). There is also a single jarring note (see on verse 5)—enough to highlight the extraordinary degree of unanimity achieved.

From Dr Kathleen Kenyon's excavations in the 1960s it seems more than probable that on the east side of the city Nehemiah's wall hugged the crest of the ridge above the Kidron gorge, whereas the earlier wall had taken a wider sweep at a lower level, near enough to the valley bottom to dominate the Gihon spring. In the new situation, with a mass of heavy debris down the valley side, with the reduced importance of the Gihon (since the development of efficient storage cisterns) and with only a small population to defend the city, Nehemiah had every reason to shorten the line and keep to the high ground. See, further, on verses 20ff.[1]

**1.** The account proceeds anti-clockwise, starting and finishing at *the Sheep Gate* (*cf.* verse 32), which we know to have been near the north-eastern corner. Its position is fixed for us by its proximity to the pool of Bethesda (Jn. 5:2), a site which has been clearly identified.

The lead given by *Eliashib* and *the priests* was decisive, and the fact that they *consecrated* their portion of the work emphasized the nature of the whole enterprise. When it was complete, the entire wall would be dedicated in a ceremony of processions, songs and sacrifices (12:27ff.). This section of the wall was near to the Temple, which lay towards the north end of the city; but the exact position of the two towers mentioned here is not yet known: only that they were points reached as one moved westward along the north wall. In fact very few of these carefully recorded points are now identifiable, since a living city offers little scope for excavation.

**2, 3.** Several of the place-names in this chapter are found also in the list of local groups of the first homecomers from exile, in Ezra 2 (reproduced in Ne. 7). The 'sons' of Jericho and of Senaah were among these (Ezr. 2:34f.), which makes it likely that *Hassenaah* in this verse is a place (*i.e.*, Senaah preceded by the definite article) rather than a person.[2]

---

[1] For fuller details see K. M. Kenyon, *Digging Up Jerusalem*, esp. pp. 89, 96, 181-187.

[2] In Ne. 11:9, however, the similar name Hassenuah is personal, or possibly descriptive (see the comment there).

**4.** The word *repaired* will now dominate the chapter. As Coggins points out, the Hebrew verb is a general term meaning 'to make firm or strong'. It does not necessarily mean restoring everything as before.

Meremoth is important, since he and Malchijah (11) provide links between the missions of Ezra and Nehemiah, which are sometimes thought to have had no common ground.[1] In Ezra 8:33 Meremoth, son of Uriah, checked in the treasure brought by Ezra from Babylon; and in Ezra 10:31, Malchijah, son of Harim, was one of those who submitted to Ezra's purge of mixed marriages. See, however, the comment on Ezra 2:61.

**5.** This is a vivid touch, a glimpse of petty pride rather than half-heartedness. The unbending *neck* is a standard picture of this unbiddable attitude (*e.g.*, Ps. 75:5, or with a different word, Ex. 32:9), and probably *their Lord* here means 'their supervisors'. (The word is plural, though it could be a plural of majesty referring to God, as RSV implies.) However, if the *nobles* cut a sorry figure (what would Amos, their townsman, have said!) the rest of their community had nothing to be ashamed of: they were responsible for two sections of the wall (see verse 27). Nor was there any support for the nobles from others of their status: see, *e.g.*, verses 9 and 12.

**7.** The end of this verse may imply that Gibeon and Mizpah were outside the boundary of Judah, and were for some reason under the direct control of the provincial governor (see on Ezr. 4:10 for the term *Beyond the River*). But the clause, *who were under the jurisdiction of*, is but one interpretation of a rather cryptic Hebrew expression.[2]

**8.** On the variety of helpers (here turning to work that was utterly unlike their own) see the opening comments on the chapter.[3]

---

[1] See Appendix IV, esp. p. 157.
[2] Heb. *lᵉkissēʾ*, lit. 'to' (or 'belonging to') 'the seat of': hence NEB, '. . . did the repairs as far as the seat of . . .'. But how likely is it that the satrap had an official residence in this up-country city? Also the chapter has no other occurrence of the preposition *lᵉ* in the sense of 'as far as' or (in a local sense) 'to'. Every such expression here represents the Heb. *ʿad*.
[3] The word for *restored* has the same form as the Heb. for 'abandoned', hence the marginal note. But it is a distinct root, whose meaning is clear, both here and at 4:2 (3:34, Heb.) and is put beyond doubt in Ex. 23:5, where it occurs three times: *viz.*, '. . . and would refrain from restoring it—you shall certainly restore it' (lit. restoring you shall restore it). There is an apparently related Ugaritic root *ʿdb*, 'prepare, set'.

**9.** Here and in verse 12 we meet two ruling officials, among the many in this chapter who put the nobles of Tekoah (5) to shame. This word for ruler is mostly translated 'prince' elsewhere in the Old Testament, although it has no royal implication. *District* basically means 'spindle', and seems to indicate the 'circle' or surrounding area rather than the city itself, and is used in connection with other towns in this chapter: see, besides verse 12, verses 14-18.

**11.** *Malchijah the son of Harim* is of special interest as a link with the activities of Ezra: see on verse 4.

**12.** See on verse 9 for this man's status. Some writers (*e.g.*, Ackroyd) have suggested that the *daughters* mean the villages in his district. But villages are only called daughters in relation to their mother-cities (as in Ezk. 16:53ff.), not in relation to their rulers. This is a genuine family effort.

**13-15.** The *Valley Gate* had been the starting-point for Nehemiah's nocturnal tour of inspection. For suggested locations of the landmarks in these three verses see the second paragraph on 2:11-15.

**16.** This *Nehemiah* is one of three people so named, including one of the first homecomers with Zerubbabel, nearly a century before (Ezr. 2:2). The name means 'Yahweh has comforted'.

*The sepulchres of David* are presumably plural to include those of his descendants. We learn from 1 Kings 2:10 that David was buried in the city that bore his name, *i.e.*, this southern part of the eastern ridge of Jerusalem. His traditional tomb, however, is on the western ridge, although the archaeological evidence is quite clear that the city of David was not on that side.[1]

The *artificial pool* is perhaps another name for 'the King's Pool' mentioned in 2:14; but another candidate for that identification is 'the Pool of Shelah of the king's garden' (3:15) if it is distinct from the pool of Siloam discussed at 2:11-15.

**17ff.** On either side of the high priest's house (20)[2] the work was done by Levites (17-19) and priests (20-22). This was a section of the east wall, but the main priestly responsibility was part of the north wall, mentioned in verse 1. The ruler of Mizpah (19) will have administered the town of that name, as distinct from the surrounding district mentioned in verse 15. *The Angle* (19f.) does not refer to a main corner of the wall, since we are still

---

[1] See, *e.g.*, K. M. Kenyon, *op. cit.*, pp. 37f.

[2] Both Baruch (20) and Meremoth (21) appear in the list of priests in 10:1-8. On Meremoth see also on verse 4 of the present chapter.

tracing the line of the eastern wall as it runs from south to north alongside the Kidron gorge; and there is soon another 'angle' in verses 24f. It may have been a projection or indentation of the wall's course, or NEB may be right in translating it 'the escarpment'.

**20ff.** It was first pointed out by Roger Dieny, a research student of the Jerusalem Ecole Biblique and a member of Dr Kenyon's 1962 excavation team, that the indications that Nehemiah shortened the building line along the east side of the city by keeping to the top of the ridge (see the second introductory paragraph to the chapter, above) may be indirectly borne out by the landmarks mentioned in these remaining verses. Private houses are from now on the chief points of reference, and where the narrative mentions city gates it is to pinpoint a position as 'opposite' one (26, 31), or 'above' another (28), not to record their repair as was the case in verses 1, 3, 6, 13, 14, 15.

**21, 22.** *Meremoth*, like a few other individuals and groups (*e.g.*, the Tekoites, verses 5 and 27), rebuilt more than one section of the wall. On his identity and its significance, see on verse 4.

**24, 25.** On the *Angle*, see on verse 19f. above.

**26, 27.** *Ophel*, meaning a swelling or eminence, was the beginning of the Temple hill, hence a convenient area for the *temple servants*, the Nethinim (see on Ezr. 2:43-54). It mounted towards the north end of this eastern ridge of Jerusalem. The *Water Gate* was presumably opposite the Gihon spring, the city's main water-supply apart from rainwater cisterns; if so, it would be a little short of halfway along the eastern wall from south to north, before reaching the beginning of the Ophel, as the end of verse 27 confirms. *The wall of Ophel* may refer to what remained of the 'outer wall ... west of Gihon, in the valley', which Manasseh 'carried ... round Ophel, and raised to a very great height' (2 Ch. 33:14). If so, it is either mentioned here as a landmark seen from above (*cf.* 'above the Horse Gate', in the next verse, 28), or else it marks the place where the old wall has climbed the valley-side to be joined by the new one.

On the *Tekoites* (27) with their double stint,[1] see on verse 5.

---

[1] There are six other mentions of double work, since 'another' means lit. 'a second', in verses 11, 19-21, 24, 30. But in most of these cases there is no mention of the original task to which 'a second' was added. (The exceptions, besides the Tekoites, are Meremoth, verses 4 and 21, and possibly Binnui (24), if the Bavvai of verse 18 is a copyist's error for his name.) So the list is evidently not exhaustive,

**31, 32.** *The corner* is a different word from 'the Angle' of verses 19f., 24f., and may perhaps mark the point at which the east wall was met by the north wall. But the word has already been used in 24b (RSV 25a), where it marked no major change of direction. Finally, however, we are brought back to the starting-point of this left-handed tour of the walls, at the *Sheep Gate* which was mentioned at the outset, to find that the high priest and his fellows (1, 2) are working side by side with the craftsmen-artists and the men of trade. It symbolizes the whole enterprise.

## Nehemiah 4. The ring of enemies

### 4:1-6. A thrust at morale

To open the attack with a barrage of words was worth trying. It is the enemy's oldest weapon, and in the form of ridicule it needs no factual ammunition; not even argument. On this occasion the morale which it attacked was too well-founded to be undermined. The words stung; but they produced not a quiver of indecision: only indignation.

**1.**[1] Rage and ridicule can be poor partners: a dismissive taunt needs coolness to be really crushing, and Sanballat's anger showed that he was more disturbed than he would admit.

**2, 3.** His contempt, therefore, was a pose, but it was well projected. He used the demagogue's techniques: a parade of the army (2a); a visiting statesman in support (3; see on 2:10); a string of rhetorical questions. It was highly effective within his own ranks, as is apparent from the contemptuous attitudes adopted towards the Jews after this (4) and from the evident enjoyment of the crowd, whose mood can be guessed from the facetiousness of Tobiah (3). Even from a man of importance, so fatuous a joke needs a little help from the atmosphere.

To look at Sanballat's questions (2) in more detail: on the rare Hebrew word for *restore*, see on 3:8. The point of *Will they sacrifice?* is probably: Are these fanatics going to *pray* the wall up? It's their only hope! *Will they finish up in a day?* I.e., have they any idea of what they are taking on? And the final question simply exaggerates the destruction, for there was plenty of usable stone.

---

and not every occurrence of 'after him/them' will necessarily mean 'immediately after'—unlike the apparently stricter expression 'next to him/them' in, *e.g.*, verses 2, 4, 5, *etc.*

[1] In the Heb. text, verses 1-6 are numbered 3:33-38, and chapter 4 (Heb.) begins at 4:7 (English).

The city gates had been burnt, but the walls had not been calcined, only broken down (1:3; 2:13).

**4, 5.** This sudden prayer, quite unannounced (in spite of GNB), transports the reader back to the very moment of dismay, as if this were an extract from the day's record, simply copied as it stood. Even if it is a more distant recollection, Nehemiah is immersed again in the experience as he writes. It is a prayer like many another in the psalms and especially Jeremiah (*e.g.*, Ps. 123 with the chilling experience of contempt; Je. 18:23 among others with the demand for retribution).[1] It is not certain whether its final phrase refers to the provoking of God (the word *thee* is not in the Heb. text) or, as in most modern versions, of the builders. But in either case it is the Lord's work that is being slighted. The Christian, while he has been shown a better answer to evil, can learn from Nehemiah to look to God, not to himself, for vindication (he was silent under the taunts), and not for a moment to accept the world's low estimate of his calling.

**6.** *So we built the wall*: the sturdy simplicity of that statement, and of the behaviour it records, makes Sanballat and his friends suddenly appear rather small and shrill, dwarfed by the faith, unity and energy of the weak. The builders' method, too, was sound in that it gave priority to closing the ring, at however modest a level, rather than to completing a number of separate sections in succession.

### 4:7-14. Resort to arms

**7, 8.** A new group, *the Ashdodites*, now joins the alliance of the north (Sanballat of Samaria), the east (Tobiah and the Ammonites) and the south (the Arabs), to bring a threat from the west as well. On the first three of these groups, see on 2:10, 19.

How much of this was mere sabre-rattling it is hard to be sure (see further on verses 11f.). The failure of this impressive group to strike a single blow suggests that 'the king's letters' (2:9) gave them pause. But their plotting, however half-hearted, clearly included potential raids and harassments (8), and had to be taken seriously.

**9.** The celebrated remark, *we prayed . . . and set a guard*, exactly reflects the faith of Nehemiah. The partnership of heaven and earth, of trust and good management, is taken for granted as

---

[1] Verse 5a, bitter though it is, should be set within the limited, this-worldly horizon of the OT, construed as a plea not for eternal damnation but for no excusing or expunging of the offence.

something normal and harmonious; and the order of precedence between them is no formality: it agrees with the preparation in chapter 1 for chapter 2, with the swifter sequence in 2 : 4f. ('so I prayed ... And I said'), and with verses 4-6 in the present chapter ('Hear, O our God ... So we built the wall'). There will be another instance in verse 14: 'Remember the Lord ... and fight'.

**10.** The picture is not idealized: the next few verses will convey the atmosphere of growing misgivings and unnerving rumours within the company, which could do as much damage as the enemy outside. Consternation over the sheer size of the task gave rise to a couplet of popular verse—for such is the saying in verse 10—which was soon on everyone's lips (note the collective term, *But Judah said*).[1] But RSV can give the wrong impression, of reluctance *to work*, whereas the Hebrew has the word *to build*, and uses the future: 'we shall not be able'. They were doubting their power to complete the task. *Cf.* NEB: '. . . we shall never be able to rebuild the wall by ourselves.' It was a natural sinking of heart, at this halfway stage; and we are reminded that dead-tiredness was not the least of their burdens.

**11-13.** The airy talk of verse 11 sounds as if it was meant for overhearing and passing on; but whether the neighbouring Jews acted as unwitting carriers of propaganda or as useful informants is difficult to say. The conspirators themselves, judging by their failure to press any attack, seem to have been in two minds between cold and hot war. Nehemiah's decisive reaction now robbed them of any initiative they had had. Intimidation had failed, and surprise was now out of the question.

The precise form of Nehemiah's defence disposition is obscure to us,[2] except that the various sectors were manned by groups which already had the natural cohesion of kinship: a characteristically simple and effective method. It also seems to have involved a temporary halt to the building, by a general call to arms instead of the mere posting of a guard as in verse 9.

---

[1] GNB commendably sets it out as verse, but the rhyming jingle it produces is not at all in character.

[2] 13a begins with 'And I stationed' (omitted in RSV), which is repeated halfway through the verse. A variant LXX reading is 'and they stood', from which NEB deduces a Heb. text 'and that they would station themselves'—making 13a refer to the enemy. But since 'behind the wall' can hardly mean outside it, the reference is evidently to the defenders. The choice of *the lowest parts* of the enclosed space was presumably dictated by the still inadequate height of the walls (*cf.*

**14.** The NEB catches the sense of the quick sequence of verbs (lit. 'And I saw and arose and said'), in the words: 'Then I surveyed the position and at once addressed the nobles ...'[1] Nehemiah's appeal shows a fine recognition of the vertical and the horizontal planes of life: *the Lord*, as ever, is the first reality for him (see on verse 9), but he is well aware that earthly ties and simple loyalties are also integral to human life and character. There is less danger of excess and distortion in the call to fight *for your brethren, ... your wives and your homes*, than in some higher-sounding, ideological battle-cry.

## 4:15–23. The fighting work-force

This is the fourth of Nehemiah's prompt counter-moves in a single chapter. He was not a man to fight new battles with old tactics. Taunts had been met by prayer and concentrated work (1–6); plots by prayer and guard-duty (7–9); stronger threats by a general call to arms and the charge to 'keep your minds on the Lord ... and fight' (10–14, *cf.* JB). Now the temporary lull is accepted for what it is: a chance to start building again, but not to disarm.

The famous sword-and-trowel exercise, which could have been a fiasco, was well thought out. Builders, needing both hands free, had swords at their belts; carriers, ranging further and risking more, needed weapons at the ready. But the heavier and longer-range equipment (16) could not be dealt with in such ways, nor could defence be simply a matter of every man fighting for himself. The answer was the shift-system for some, and the posting of officers as described in verse 16, unified by a single commander and clear communication (18b–20). But to Nehemiah these were no more than workmanlike precautions of limited value. His confidence went deeper: *Our God will fight for us* (20). He knew the truth of Psalm 127: 'Unless the Lord builds ... Unless the Lord watches over the city ... It is in vain.'

---

verse 6), and the *open* places (or 'bare rock') by the need for mobility unhampered by rubble or buildings. JB puts it well with 'positions down behind the wall where the place was clear'. GNB interprets the 'open places' as gaps in the wall, which is reconcilable with 4 : 6 since the gates were not yet up (6 : 1); but if so, it could have been expressed more clearly.

[1] JB 'I had seen their fear' (*cf.* GNB) assumes that the word 'fear' has accidentally dropped out of the text because of the similarity between 'to see' (*r' h*) and 'to fear' (*yr'*). But the similarity is chiefly present in the 3rd person of the imperfect, not between 'I saw' (*'ēre'*) and 'their fear' (*yir'āṯām*).

**21, 22.** The final paragraph shows that the threats and counter-measures have had a bracing effect, dispelling the tiredness and despondency of verse 10. Every minute of daylight was now precious, and darkness must not undo the day's achievements. The danger of leaving Jerusalem an almost empty shell was a recurrent concern to Nehemiah: see 7:4; 11:1, 2.

**23.** Nehemiah emerges here as a leader in the further sense that he set a strong example of what he had urged others to do (*cf.* the previous verse). He was not an egalitarian, but used his special resources to make his contribution the more effective. The next chapter will show other and more striking instances of this.

The last few words of this verse are unintelligible in the Hebrew as it stands, which reads 'each his weapon the water'. Most modern versions emend *ha-mayim* (the water) to *bᵉyāḏô* (in his hand) or far less drastically to *hêmîn* (he had at/in his right hand; *cf.* NEB). The latter seems the best of many suggestions.[1]

### Nehemiah 5. A threat from within

In this chapter the enemies and the city walls recede from view, to reveal a more subtle problem. Here the menace is hunger and exploitation, and the structure at risk is the community itself. The chapter may be a digression, a calculated preview of later and deeper troubles, to balance the recent emphasis on military threats and on the loyalty which they evoked, and to show another aspect of Nehemiah's burdens and his leadership. Certainly the final paragraph takes us twelve years further on.

But verses 1-13 may well be chronologically as well as topically in place. While the few weeks of rebuilding seem certainly too short a time for these developments (the whole enterprise took only fifty-two days, 6:15), Judah's post-exilic history had not begun with Nehemiah's arrival, nor even with the 'great trouble and shame' which were reported to him in Susa. His diverting of manpower from raising crops to raising walls may have been the final burden; it did not have to be the first.

---

[1] AV, 'saving that every one put them off for washing', follows the Vulg. which interprets *šilḥô* (his weapon, RSV) as a verb, 'he let it go', *i.e.*, 'discarded it'. But this leaves several words to be mentally supplied; so too does RV, 'every one went with his weapon to the water'.

**5:1-5. A great outcry**

The hidden strains within the community, masked by the concerted defence effort (if they belonged to this period—see above), needed bringing to the surface, like, *e.g.*, those of the early church (*cf.* Acts 6:1); and in this case, as in the other, thanks to fine leadership, nothing but good was to come of the exposure. Incidentally it emerges that the wives could take some credit for the protest (1).

The troubles were real enough. Verse 2 reveals a natural tendency to argue that too much was being sacrificed to Nehemiah's project.[1] 'After all', as such citizens might have put it, 'you can't eat walls.' In verses 3 and 4 the underlying seriousness of the position comes to light—for when a small-holder has to part with the title-deeds to raise money for seed-corn and taxes, he is all but doomed. Even so, verse 5 administers a double shock in revealing not only the end of that road, the sale of a man's children, but the identity (*our brethren*) of those who had forced this on their victims.

**5:6-13. A wrong redressed**

Nehemiah, fortunately for his people, was far from unshockable. His anger was the measure of his concern, or love, as was our Lord's in, *e.g.*, Mark 3:5; John 2:14ff.; or Paul's in 2 Corinthians 11:29. But the same concern made it controlled and constructive, as the passage goes on to show.

**7.** NEB has the rather striking translation, 'I mastered my feelings and reasoned with the nobles...'; but RSV is more likely to be right with *I took counsel with myself,*[2] *and I brought charges....* The second of these verbs has strong associations with legal proceedings. The *great assembly*[3] would add powerful pressure to the charges.

But what exactly was the reproach in verse 7? Levying interest (RSV)? Imposing burdens (JB, *cf.* GNB)? The normal word for 'interest' (*cf.* Dt. 23:19f.) is not used here, and 'imposing

[1] JB, NEB adopt the conjecture that a consonant has dropped out before 'many' (*rbym*), and therefore read 'we are mortgaging (*'rbym*) our sons... to get grain'. This is very plausible, but textually unsupported.
[2] 'Took counsel' treats the root *mlk* as having a sense found in Aramaic. 'Mastered' identifies it with the verb 'to reign', but this would be the only occurrence of that verb in the niph˙al conjugation. A different verb is used in Pr. 16:32 for ruling one's spirit.
[3] NEB, for no sufficient reason, finds no reference to this in the Heb. But *qᵉhillâ* clearly means 'assembly' in Dt. 33:4.

burdens'[1] is out of step with the Hebrew of verse 10. The terms here and in verse 10 mean, at their simplest, 'lending' (not 'exacting') and 'a loan' (not 'interest'). But the words implied a strict business relationship (*cf.* the Heb. of 1 Sa. 22:2), and Nehemiah's charge is therefore that (in our terms) the lenders were behaving like pawnbrokers—and harsh ones at that—instead of like brothers. They were lending only with the best of cover (*cf.* NEB) and, in their case, with the worst of motives. It was quite legal to demand a material pledge against a loan (*cf.*, *e.g.*, Dt. 24:10-13), and Nehemiah himself had probably exercised this right (see on verse 10). But in hard times legal rights, to say nothing of wrongs, can deal mortal blows.

**8.** Brought out into the open (*cf.* Mk 9:33f.), and measured against generous actions, the smart deals now looked impossibly shabby, even to the dealers themselves. In this verse Nehemiah harps relentlessly on buying and selling, and it makes little difference to his arguments whether he is describing what he and others had done for Jewish slaves abroad or for those who fell into gentile hands at home—except that in the latter case some of the very people now sold back[2] by gentiles had first been traded to them by Jews.

**9.** Their shame allows him to take higher ground; and it is not only a heightening of the charge (that of bringing God himself into contempt) but an appeal to higher motives. There is invitation as well as reproach in his *Ought you not* . . .? or more simply 'Will you not . . .?'

**10.** Now, disarmingly, Nehemiah includes himself in the charge.[3] Quite clearly (judging by his shocked reaction in verse 6) his own lending had been on very different terms from theirs, but he sees now that the depth of poverty had called for gifts, not loans, and he makes no disclaimers—except indirectly by the

---

[1] This translation involves a slight change in two Heb. words in verse 7 (altering the letter *š* to *s*) but inconsistently leaving them intact when they recur in verse 10. A further difficulty is that (*pace* Rudolph) *maśśā'* . . . *nōš'îm*, as proposed for verse 7, would more naturally mean bearing a burden than imposing one.

[2] RSV, *that they may be sold to us*, is faithful to the Heb. text, whereas GNB alters 'us' to 'you'.

[3] Some commentators take Nehemiah to be still contrasting his generosity with the harshness of others. But he uses of himself the terms he has condemned in verse 7, and his final plea here (10b) renounces the 'lending' which he acknowledged earlier in the verse. The noun is cognate with the verb, and both, in my view, mean lending (see on verse 7), *i.e.*, lending on security.

change from 'I' and 'us' in this verse to 'you' in the next, as truth demanded.

**11-13.** Ever realistic, Nehemiah leaves no room for post-ponement or for second thoughts, and makes sure that the promises are upgraded into oaths, properly sworn in the presence of the priests. Not content with that, he performs what is far more than a visual aid: a self-fulfilling act of conditional judgment, comparable to those of the prophets (*e.g.*, 2 Ki. 13:15-19; Je. 19:10ff.). *Cf.*, in the New Testament, Paul's similar gesture in Acts 18:6, and our Lord's instructions to His envoys in Matthew 10:14f. We may be inclined to picture the enthusiastic response in 13b as that of *the assembly* apart from and against the guilty minority (*cf.* 7c); but the final statement speaks of a general obedience (*the people*), perhaps implying that like Nehemiah himself (10), others besides the chief offenders had discovered adjustments to be made (*cf.* 10), and found joy in doing the right thing at last.

*Note.* In verse 11 *the hundredth* would be a surprisingly low return on capital, but the reckoning may be in monthly terms (*i.e.*, 12 per cent per annum). The demand in this half of the verse is for a refund either of interest charged on the loans (*cf.* RSV), or (as I prefer) of the income derived by the creditors from the property they have taken in pledge (*cf.* NEB: 'Give back today to your debtors their fields and vineyards . . ., as well as the income in money, and in corn . . .'). The word *hundredth* (*mᵉʾat̠*) could presumably denote this yield, and fix the assessment of it; but some have conjectured that the letter ś or š has dropped out of this word, implying either *maśśᵉʾat̠* (burden, tribute; here taken to mean the proceeds from the confiscated fields and vineyards),[1] or else *maśśᵉʾat̠*, 'loan' (on pledge), hence 'debt' (*cf.* JB: 'Return them their fields . . . forthwith, and remit the debt on the money, corn, wine and oil which you have lent them').

A central task for the translator, throughout this passage, is to give a self-consistent interpretation of the closely related words rendered in RSV by the terms 'exacting', 'interest' and 'lending', in verses 7, 10 and 11. See the comments on verses 7 and 10.

## 5:14-19. A pattern of leadership
The story of the crisis, just told, and especially the part played in

---

[1] This is how NEB arrives at the word 'income'; but the textual conjecture may not be necessary.

it by Nehemiah's example (10), makes this a suitable moment for him to pause and describe his style of government.

It is here (14) that we learn his official status as *governor*,[1] and the length of his first term of office, *i.e.*, from 445 to 433 BC. Some events of his second term, or visit, are described with considerable animation in 13:6-31.

*The food allowance* (14, 18), although assigned to him by higher authority, would have been a charge on the local population; and just how big a charge emerges in the hospitality account set out in verses 17 and 18. That Nehemiah should have shouldered all this himself is proof—if such were needed—that to him the whole enterprise was a labour of love.

He reveals his twofold motivation: first, filial reverence for God, which restrained him from 'lording it over the people' (15b), and made heaven's verdict all-important to him (19); and second, brotherly compassion, 'because the servitude was heavy upon this people' (18). In his own brusque style he exemplified the two great commandments, and anticipated the cheerful disregard of one's entitlements which Paul would expound in 1 Corinthians 9.

## Nehemiah 6. The enemy outfaced

### 6:1-9. Five messages from Sanballat

The defence works had now reached that crucial stage, on the very brink of completion, at which all could still be lost or soon be won. The open gateways (1) were the enemy's last hope of regaining the upper hand without actually mounting a siege, which would be out of the question against fellow subjects of Persia.

**2, 3.** On the power wielded by *Sanballat, Tobiah* (verse 1) and *Geshem*, see the comments on 2:10, 19. The suggestion of *the plain of Ono*[2] was plausible, for it was about equidistant from Samaria and Jerusalem. At the same time, it was for Nehemiah more than a day's journey from his city, and (as Brockington points out) at

---

[1] The word used in this passage and in most others is *peḥâ*, derived from Akkadian. The Persian equivalent, transliterated in RV as the Tirshatha, is used of Nehemiah in 8:9; 10:1; and occurs also in Ezr. 2:63 (where see note); Ne. 7:65, 70 (69 Heb.).

[2] The expression, (*one of*) *the villages*, seems a little vague, and the word translated 'villages' is not the normal plural. NEB, JB may well be right in taking it as an actual name, Hakkephirim. A similar name (spelt Chephirah in RSV) occurs in 7:29, and the town of Ono in 7:37.

the very limit of his territory to the north-west, bordering the districts of both Samaria and Ashdod. Since both of these were hostile regions (*cf.* 4:2, 7) the plan smelt of treachery. At best, the journey would have wasted precious days; therefore wisely enough he based his refusal on this, rather than on his suspicions. Incidentally, the familiar translation in RSV (following AV, RV), *I am doing a great work*, may seem to smack of self-praise. The sense comes across better in, *e.g.*, NEB: 'I have important work on my hands', or still more objectively, '. . . a huge task . . .'.

**4-9.** By the fourth time of asking, Sanballat must have realized that his anxiety was beginning to show through. His change of tactics, the sending of an open letter, ensured that the malicious rumours it contained would sooner or later be public property, and that Nehemiah would realize this. It would take some courage to brush the whole thing aside, and indeed verse 9 confirms the fact by its urgent little prayer.

### 6:10-14. Hired prophets use their influence

The prophet Shemaiah (who is otherwise unknown to us, though he may have been connected with the Delaiah family mentioned in Ezr. 2:60) used all his arts in this encounter. His confinement to his house[1] made a convenient opportunity to request Nehemiah to come to him, instead of his going to Nehemiah; for this important visitor would be noticed, and his visit construed as a search for guidance and a sign of uncertainty. The fact that Shemaiah would propose going to the Temple shows that his disability, if it existed at all, was only temporary, hardly a sufficient reason to bring the governor to his house.[2]

Having secured the interview, the prophet dressed up his proposal as an oracle, in something akin to verse, so that its form would be as compelling as its content. JB sets it out in separate lines, ending with the couplet:

> 'for they are coming to kill you,
> they are coming to kill you tonight.'[3]

**11.** Nehemiah's spirited retort shows a proper pride and a

---

[1] This was presumably through some ritual defilement, as in, *e.g.*, Nu. 19:11ff., rather than the house-arrest which Jeremiah may have been describing in Je. 36:5 by the same Heb. word, '*āṣûr*, 'confined'.

[2] Kellermann's conjecture that Nehemiah was of royal blood (*cf.* verse 7), and that Shemaiah was planning a secret coronation, is discussed on p. 171.

[3] 'By night' would be more accurate.

proper humility. An equivalent of the former is spelt out finely by Joseph in Genesis 39:8f., by Jesus in Luke 13:31-33, and by Paul in Acts 21:10-14. The latter quality, a proper humility, speaks out here in RSV (*cf.* NEB): '*And what man such as I could go into the temple and live?*'[1]—for Nehemiah was no priest, and had no right of access to the temple itself (as distinct from the surrounding courtyards). King Uzziah, trespassing, had been fortunate to escape with no more than leprosy (2 Ch. 26:16ff.; *cf.* Nu. 18:7). Nehemiah, had he tried to save himself in such a way, would have lost, possibly, his life, certainly his honour; and would have jeopardized the very cause he had at heart.

**12, 13.** The right decision had been swiftly made, on principles that were stronger than the apparent situation or the fear of death. It was this, not any flaw in the prophet's technique, that enabled Nehemiah on reflection to see through the whole stratagem, from its source to its intended outcome.

**14.** This interjection is, apart from the more elaborate prayer of 4:4f., the first in a series of swift appeals to God (truly appealing, in more senses than one) found elsewhere at 5:19 and 13:14, 22, 29, 31. What they have in common is a resolve to do the right thing and leave the outcome, whether reward or punishment, to heaven. They are discussed further on pp. 168f.

We learn here, quite in passing, that Shemaiah's was only one voice in an impressive chorus of discouragement. And the mention of Noadiah furnishes a reminder that prophetesses, good and bad, were not as uncommon in Old Testament times as one might imagine. Miriam, Deborah and Huldah are honourable examples, while Noadiah had some evil predecessors, who mixed magic and money-making with their prophesying in Ezekiel's day (Ezk. 13:17-23).

### 6:15-19. Triumph and chagrin

After the high emotions on both sides, there is a pleasing dryness about the words, *So the wall was finished.* . . . It recalls the sequel in chapter 4 to the enemy's opening salvo of abuse: the quiet report, after an initial outburst of indignation, 'So we built the wall . . .' (4:6). The operation was, throughout, a triumph of concentration amidst every kind of distraction. Its speed is measured by the fact that *Elul* was the sixth month of the year, which began

---

[1] The alternative translation is also possible, but a little forced: '. . . would go into the temple to save his life?' (AV, RV; *cf.* JB, GNB).

with Nisan (2:1) in the spring. Into that time Nehemiah had crowded all the events of chapters 2 to 6.

**16.** The sense in which the surrounding people *were afraid*[1] would be that they were awed, rather than apprehensive. Their respect for the Jews and their God was increased, and their self-esteem diminished.[2] So the very size of the circle which Sanballat had managed to draw round Jerusalem (see on 4:7) brought all the wider recognition of God's power. *Cf., e.g.*, Paul's experience of the fruits of persecution in Philippians 1:12ff.

**17-19.** While chapter 5 brought to light the severe strains beneath the temporary unity, these three verses reveal a still more serious threat in the disloyalties that might have sabotaged the whole enterprise, and which would persist to the end of Nehemiah's story (see the final chapter).

This evil, like the other, found its foothold in the more prosperous levels of society, this time through the love of power and status rather than primarily through love of money. *Tobiah* was a more insidious influence in this respect than Sanballat, since he was probably a fellow-Jew, in addition to being (as his own and his son's names indicate) a nominal adherent of Yahweh.[3] His numerous binding agreements (*by oath*, 18) within the Jewish community were probably trading contracts, facilitated by his marriage connections. His wife's family, the descendants of *Arah*, is mentioned in Ezra 2:5, and while neither *Shecaniah* nor this *Meshullam* can be identified, we know from 13:4 that Tobiah had family ties with the priestly or high-priestly house of Eliashib, probably by marriage. While such links and loyalties were embarrassing enough in themselves, we now learn how busily they were exploited by intrigues, persuasive talk, leaks of information and threatening letters. All this, in addition to the outside pressures already described, brought Nehemiah under attack from almost every quarter. It had been a test worthy of the man, and it was not yet over.

---

[1] The alternative reading, 'they saw', is equally possible, but not so likely, in that it is less vigorous.

[2] NEB (*cf.* JB) changes a consonant and some vowels to read *wayyippālē'* ('and it was wonderful') instead of *wayyippᵉlû* ('and they fell'). This is attractively easy, but unnecessary.

[3] See on 2:10. His son's name, Jehohanan ('Yahweh has shown mercy'), became increasingly common among Jews, and in the NT it is familiar to us in our spelling of it as John.

## Nehemiah 7. After the city the citizens

Most of this chapter is an extract from the archives, for the purpose shown in verse 5: to make sure of the city's continuity with the past. So verses 6 to the end copy out the whole of Ezra 2, the list of the first repatriates from exile, and of their origins.

### 7:1-4. First steps towards community

**1.** The opening words glance back at the two last stages of re-fortifying which were noted in 6 : 1 and 15, seeing them as a base for further progress, not as an end in themselves. Nor was the community to be an end in itself. Along with the *gatekeepers* (*i.e.*, guardians of the city gates, not those of the Temple, *cf.* verse 3), the *singers* and (other) *Levites* shared the priority, since worship was Jerusalem's *raison d'être*.[1]

**2.** *My brother Hanani* was the one whose sad news of Jerusalem had set in motion the whole course of Nehemiah's actions, back in Susa (1 : 2). Had that long journey to the royal capital been in fact a covert deputation, in hopes of just such an outcome? If so, it marked Hanani as a man of initiative and leadership, like his brother or kinsman. In Nehemiah's judgment, *Hananiah's* decisive qualification to share authority with Hanani was his character and outlook. Professional competence, vital though it was, and implied by the position he already held, was not enough in itself, in view of the divided loyalties of so many leading citizens (6 : 17–19). *The castle* (*bîrâ*) is the same word as 'the fortress' in 2 : 8, which speaks of 'the fortress of the temple', possibly the tower of Hananel (3 : 1) on the Temple mount.

**3, 4.** If there was a temptation to rely on walls and gates, Nehemiah (or Hananiah[2]) was proof against it. The Jebusites had made that error (2 Sa. 5 : 6), forgetting that the final strength or weakness of a city is its people. But the Hebrew of verse 3a is obscure. While it obviously speaks of extra precautions, these may refer either to the midday siesta (NEB, 'not to be left open during the heat of the day . . . while the gatekeepers are standing

---

[1] NEB and some commentators omit the *singers* and *Levites*, considering them an insertion by a copyist who took the gatekeepers to be levitical guardians of the Temple, like those of verse 45 (*cf.* 1 Ch. 9 : 17, 23), and who therefore added the other levitical orders to the list, as in 43f. But this is a conjecture, without textual support.

[2] The consonantal text of verse 3 reads 'And he said . . .'. Traditionally this is taken to be an error for 'And I said . . .'; but these instructions could quite well be those of the military leader mentioned just above.

at ease'[1]) or, more probably, to the morning and evening routine, directing that the gates should be opened late and closed early (*cf.* RSV, GNB). The further precaution of enrolling civilian guards was realistic in its posting of them to defend what mattered to them most, even though their homes were little more than ruins waiting to be rebuilt (*cf.* 3b with 4b).

### 7:5-73. The quest for continuity

**5.** Of all biblical characters, Nehemiah is perhaps the most explicit on 'the practice of the presence of God'. Here his sense of being divinely prompted (5a) to summon the people for enrolment was to be borne out by the events it set in motion, namely the heart-searchings and re-dedication to be recounted in chapters 8–10. Meanwhile his immediate concern was to get his people rightly orientated, sure both of their inheritance and their calling.

**6–73.** These verses are therefore an almost exact transcription of Ezra 2. The occasional divergences are generally agreed to have arisen in the copying; there are notes on the chief examples of this in the Ezra commentary on that chapter.

## Nehemiah 8. The reading of the law

Ezra now makes his first appearance in this book, to play a leading role in the realm of law and covenant.[2] For several chapters Nehemiah's memoirs will give place to records in the third person. Then he will take up the story again himself with the dedication of the city wall (12:27ff.) and, in the final chapter, with the account of his running battle against all things foreign.

### 8:1-8. The great assembly

The chapter should probably begin, as in RSV's paragraphing, with the second half of 7:73. There is a smooth transition from the old record of Ezra 2, copied out in Nehemiah 7, to the scene which now unfolds, since both introduce us to a great assembly at Jerusalem in the seventh month, the crown of the year.

---

[1] Lit. 'standing'. This can denote inactivity, but such a meaning is more likely when 'stand' is set in contrast to 'pass on' or to some other verb of action: *e.g.* 1 Sa. 9:27; 2 Ki. 13:18 (Heb.).

[2] In 1 Esdras, a fragment corresponding to our verses 1–13a follows straight on from the equivalent of Ezr. 10:44. For opinions on the significance of this, see Appendix IV, pp. 150f.

Nehemiah had lost no time: the wall had been completed only a few days before this (6:15; 8:2), yet a sizeable platform had meanwhile been constructed for the great occasion (4).

**1.** There was a mood of rare responsiveness, shown not only in the people's flocking to Jerusalem *as one man* (just as their forefathers had gathered after the Return: Ezr. 3:1), but in their call for Ezra to read out the Scripture to them. Although this was not a sudden impulse—the platform was ready for him—it was clearly a general desire, and in that sense spontaneous, not a formality imposed by the leadership. The attentive listening (3) and the heart-searching that ensued (9) gave further evidence of it.

So Ezra now emerges from obscurity, and it is typical of him that he has quietly waited to be asked for: *cf.* his earlier withdrawals, so powerful in their influence, in Ezra 9:3ff.; 10:1, 6.

For all its ordinariness, the expression, *the book of the law of Moses which the Lord had given to Israel*, makes two important and contested points: first, that what the people called for, and what Ezra ostensibly produced, was no new manifesto but the foundation articles of the faith, laid down at the Exodus; secondly that these were credited with full divine authority.[1] *The Lord had given* is literally 'the Lord had commanded'; and one does not tamper with material that one would describe in such terms. This would hardly need saying but for the widely held hypothesis (popularized by Wellhausen in the 1870s) that Ezra's law book was a revision and rewriting of tradition, Mosaic in name and, arguably, in spirit, but not in fact. To accept this view is to conclude, however charitably one may express it, that Ezra committed a pious fraud that day, passing off his improved version as the original which had been called for; not only 'mending the oracles of God' but reading aloud their repeated warnings (Dt. 4:2; 12:32) against doing such a thing.[2]

**2.** *Ezra the priest* is given his fuller description in verse 9 as 'priest and scribe', and his impressive qualifications for both these titles in Ezra 7:1-6.[3] As for the assembly, it is no small

---

[1] *Cf.*, *e.g.*, Rudolph, pp. 145, 149.
[2] See further the section 'Ezra's book of the law', below, Appendix V, pp. 158-164.
[3] He thereby fulfilled the true but neglected calling of the priesthood to *teach*, not only to worship. Note the order in which these two functions appear in Dt. 33:10, and the prominence given to teaching in Mal. 2:6-9.

matter that it consisted not of men only, nor adults only, but of *all who could hear with understanding*. The law had always envisaged 'a wise and understanding people', taught from childhood not only the words of God but what the words and rituals meant (Ex. 12:26f.; Dt. 4:6; 6:6ff.; 31:12f.). Mindless superstition was the mark of paganism ('they cannot understand', Is. 44:18f.), and had been the downfall of an apostate Israel (Ho. 4:6: 'My people are destroyed for lack of knowledge').

**3.** *The Water Gate* was on the east side of the city (3:26), giving access to the principal spring, the Gihon, in the valley below. It is interesting that this assembly, unlike that of Ezra 3:1ff., was not held in the Temple court, where the altar was the focal point, but at one of the centres of city life, the kind of place where God's wisdom pleads most urgently to be heard (*cf.* Pr. 1:20f.; 8:1ff.). The law itself insisted that its voice must not be confined to the sanctuary but heard in the house and the street (Dt. 6:7ff.).

It would be a mistake to try to reckon how much of the Pentateuch Ezra could have read in this long morning, since his prime concern was to give the people a grasp of the message. Notice the stress on understanding, in verses 2, 3, 7, 8, 12. On the general attentiveness, see the comment on verse 1.

**4.** The *pulpit* (lit. 'tower') was a platform large enough to accommodate Ezra and his thirteen helpers, and high enough to dominate the scene. These thirteen may well have been priests; and there is a further company of thirteen named in verse 7.[1]

It is not clear exactly how these groups operated, but we may surmise that those on the platform successively read out portions of the law (as, in the synagogue, seven or more readers might share this task on the sabbath), and that the thirteen, or more,[2] of verse 7 moved among the congregation in the intervals between these readings, making sure that they were understood. See further, on verses 7 and 8.

**5.** The formal display and opening of the sacred scroll has its counterpart in the synagogue; but whether such points in common originated with this occasion or preceded it, or arose independently, can only be matters of conjecture. What is strikingly apparent is the royal reception given to the Word of

---

[1] 1 Esdras 9:43f. differs over some of the names in our verse 4, and places seven on Ezra's right and six on his left, in contrast to our text.

[2] The Heb. text of verse 7 makes the Levites *additional* to the men who are named there (see RSV mg. and AV, RV); but 1 Esdras 9:48 may be correct in omitting the 'and', as RSV and most modern versions consider.

God. This day was to prove a turning-point. From now on, the Jews would be predominantly 'the people of a book'. At the dedication of Solomon's Temple there had been glory and beauty, natural and supernatural, to overwhelm the worshippers. Here the focus, apart from a wooden platform, was a scroll—or more exactly, what was written in it. Its opening brought the people to their feet.

**6.** This verse and the next two rule out any thought of bibliolatry as though the scroll were being venerated simply as a relic. The adoration was for God, and the attitudes were eloquent of some of the main facets of worship: salutation, or yearning, by the uplifted hands; self-abasement, or entreaty, by the gesture of prostration.

**7.** The remark that *the people remained in their places* may imply that the thirteen instructors who are named here (not to be confused with the thirteen on the platform; see the comment and second footnote on verse 4) were free to move around amongst them, explaining and expounding.

**8.** While we cannot be certain of the details, the first half of this verse, which is concerned with the reading, may refer to what Ezra and his companions on the rostrum did, while the second half brings us back to the crowd and the teaching officers. Much depends on the word *clearly*, which JB and GNB take to mean 'translating it', although this would be an unusual meaning of the word. Certainly an oral translation into Aramaic became the established custom in due course (the Targums are the written versions of this), but we cannot be sure that it began as early as this. Indeed, Nehemiah's indignation at finding families which 'could not speak the language of Judah', on his second visit to Jerusalem about twelve years later, suggests that in his first term of office he could expect Hebrew to be generally understood.[1]

The basic meaning of the word in question is 'to make distinct or separate', which could denote either that the reading was well articulated or that the law was read and expounded section by section.[2] Either of these would be appropriate; probably both were true. The whole occasion emphasizes the clarity and candour of God's dealings with His people, and, not least, the

---

[1] See 13:6f., 23ff. On the Nehemiah-Ezra chronology, which would re-date the present chapter and make the above argument irrelevant, see Appendix IV, pp. 146ff.

[2] The word 'parasha', the Massoretes' term for a paragraph of the Pentateuch, comes from this root.

contrast drawn elsewhere between His ministers and 'the mediums and the wizards who chirp and mutter' (*cf.* Is. 8:19f.).

## 8:9-12. A call to festivity

Three times in this short paragraph it is pointed out that holiness and gloom go ill together. What makes it rather striking, to our ears, is the calm assumption that this should go without saying. True, the Day of Atonement, with its call to 'afflict' oneself, was holy (Lv. 23:27), but it existed to clear the air for happier occasions. To be 'altogether joyful' was the prospect held before the guests of God (Dt. 16:15), and the words that went most naturally with 'holiness' were not only 'justice and righteousness' but 'glory', 'beauty', 'strength' and 'joy'.[1]

**9.** *Nehemiah*, whose presence during the 'teach-in' the reader will have assumed,[2] characteristically takes the lead now. The fact that the day was *holy* is confirmed by Leviticus 23:24. On the festive implications of this, see the paragraph above.

**10.** It was equally typical of Nehemiah to spell the matter out with immediate and creative suggestions. What he urged on them took account of elementary facts of life: the little luxuries that can turn a meal into a feast,[3] but also the caring and love which can turn simple gaiety into *the joy of the Lord*—a joy which is invigorating, not escapist or evanescent. Nehemiah's concern for those *for whom nothing is prepared* was well rooted in his own outlook and practice: *cf.* 5:14-19.

**11.** *So the Levites . . .*: better, 'The Levites too were quietening the people . . .', though their soothing words had none of the imaginative force of Nehemiah's. The layman, not for the first or last time, had shown a surer grasp of reality than the professionals.

**12.** Once more, in the final words, we are brought to the heart of the matter. The completed walls, the throng and the conviviality were all peripheral or secondary. To have *understood* what God was saying was what made the occasion. It was a step from blind religiousness towards some degree of divine-human

---

[1] See, *e.g.*, Pss. 96; 99; Is. 35.

[2] Those who, on other grounds, hold that Ezra and Nehemiah were not contemporaries have to excise Nehemiah's name from this verse. For a critique of their reasons see pp. 148ff.

[3] There was, incidentally, no contravention of the law of Lv. 3:17 in Nehemiah's exhortation to 'eat the fat'. The word he used means 'rich food', not the forbidden animal-fat of the levitical law.

fellowship. Its full flowering would be in the new covenant with its assurance, 'they shall all know me'; but the old covenant already held much promise of its successor.

## 8:13-18. The feast of tabernacles

**13.** After the extensive teaching session came the intensive one, which shows how seriously the emphasis on Scripture was being taken. The expression, *to study the words of the law*, suggests something more than passive listening. As *heads of fathers' houses*, these were the men to spread the knowledge of Scripture throughout the families within their clans, if the ideal of Deuteronomy 6:6ff. was to be realized. It could not all be left to the priests and Levites.

**14, 15.** We get the impression that the rules for the feast, found in Leviticus 23:39-43, now came as something of a discovery. Not that the festival itself had fallen out of use 'from the days of Jeshua' (17)—see, *e.g.*, Ezra 3:4—but rather, that its camping-out element had meanwhile lapsed or been reduced to a mere token. The feast had two sides to it: it was a vintage festival, the 'ingathering at the year's end' (Ex. 34:22), but also a memorial of the wilderness, when God had 'made the people of Israel dwell in booths' (Lv. 23:43). It seems to have been this aspect that had fallen into neglect. Custom, as happens so often in religious history, had overlaid and modified 'the faith once delivered to the saints', so that the freshly studied Scripture, like a cleaned painting, now revealed some long-forgotten colours.

**16, 17.** There was nearly a fortnight in which to 'publish and proclaim' (15) the preparations for the feast, whose appointed date was the fifteenth of the month. Meanwhile, on the tenth, the law had prescribed the Day of Atonement (Lv. 16:29ff.; 23:27ff.). Our passage makes no mention of it, presumably because it did not involve a general pilgrimage to Jerusalem, for the concern of chapters 8-10 is with gatherings of the whole people. The special fast day of chapters 9 and 10, held before the crowds had finally dispersed from the festival, was more significant than this for the progress of the story, culminating as it did in the national covenant.[1]

The strange blend of settled and unsettled life, presented by

---

[1] Some commentators have argued, from the silence of the narrative, that Ezra's law book contained as yet no mention of the Day of Atonement, or else no mention of its date. This requires the view that the Pentateuch was a slowly

the incongruous sight of shanties perched on the roofs of houses and filling the city squares, was a forcible reminder, experienced for a whole week, of pilgrim conditions and the miraculous journey to the promised land. There was now a second Exodus to reinforce the message, and the reference in verse 17 to ancient history and to the more recent return from captivity suggests that the point was taken.

On matters of detail: the two squares may well have been the nearest to the Temple area, which was the Ophel mount at the north-east end of the city, since the *Water Gate* was about half way along the eastern wall (*cf.* 3:26) and the *Gate of Ephraim* must have been on the north side, looking towards the territory which gave it its name. On the middle clause of verse 17 see the comments on verses 14 and 15, above.

**18.** The scattered regulations for the festival were all searched out and followed with a will. Verse 15 has taken up the instruction given in Leviticus 23:40ff. to gather leafy branches; the last sentence of verse 17 chimes in with the note of *rejoicing* called for in Deuteronomy 16:13-15; and now we learn of the reading of *the law* prescribed in Deuteronomy 31:10-13 for every seventh year, and of the *solemn assembly* of Numbers 29:35. Whether this occasion coincided with the seventh year, the year of release (as A. Pavlovský contends: *Biblica* 38 (1957), pp. 273-305, 428-456), or whether Ezra was going beyond the minimum requirement of the law and introducing an annual reading, there is no means of knowing; but such became the custom in due course.

So the move to make Scripture the guiding principle of Jewish life was powerfully initiated. The great teaching operation on the first day of the month, the training session which had followed it, and now the seven days of readings at the festival had exposed the people to the fundamentals of their faith with considerable thoroughness. But the clinching of it was yet to come, as the next two chapters will show.

### Nehemiah 9:1-37. The great confession

This chapter flows straight on into chapter 10 (which begins in

---

evolving document (though it is generally agreed that the Day of Atonement shows very ancient features), but in itself the suggestion is as precarious as are all arguments from silence. See also the concluding comment on verse 1, above.

the Heb. Bible at our verse 38) where the prolonged heart-searching culminates in a series of specific pledges.

## 9:1-5. The six-hour service

**1.** The timing of this act of penitence, *on the twenty-fourth day of this month*, is of some interest, first because it reverses the sequence we might have expected, by putting the fasting after the feasting of chapter 8, and secondly because it allowed a day's interval between the two occasions. The feast had finished on the twenty-second; those who stayed on were doing so by deliberate choice. As for the sequence, Nehemiah's quick reaction against a tearful response to the law at its earlier reading (8:9-12) shows that he was profoundly eager to associate God's will with delight (as the psalmists did: *e.g.*, Pss. 19:7ff.; 40:8; 119:14, 16, *etc.*). But now it was equally important to set this delight firmly in contrast to the gall of sin, and to face the facts of the past and the challenge of the future. So at this turning-point in the people's history, the seven-day feast must leave behind it something more durable than a sweet taste in the mouth. The responsive mood must be harnessed to the will. And, with the realism of that culture, the body and its attire must express the same self-humbling and sorrow as would the words and tone of voice.

**2.** The repeated readings from the law were bearing fruit. The words *separated . . . from all foreigners* reflect the emphasis of, *e.g.*, Leviticus 20:26, 'I . . . have separated you from the peoples, that you should be mine.' The acceptance of this, in the straitened circumstances of the time, implied a spirit of dedication rather than arrogance, for the neighbouring gentiles were socially well worth cultivating (*cf.* 6:17f.). See also the comment on Ezra 6:21.

The sense of solidarity in guilt, expressed here, is often found in the Old Testament (*e.g.* Ne. 1:6; Ps. 106:6), and is only spoken against when it is used to question God's justice, or to cut the nerve of personal responsibility (Ezk. 18, *passim*).

**3.** Once again the book of the law is basic to the day's proceedings. Its teachings will have both evoked and informed the three hours of worship which followed the three hours of reading. In the light of the previous chapter we may take it that the reading was no mere stream of words, but punctuated with explanatory comments and applications to the present situation.

**4, 5.** *The stairs of the Levites* may have been steps from one courtyard of the Temple to another (such as the fifteen steps leading from the court of the women to the court of Israel, upon which, in the Herodian Temple complex, 'the Levites used to sing', according to the Mishnah[1]). Or, since we are not told where this assembly took place, the word translated stairs (lit. 'the ascent') may refer to the platform of 8:4 (JB, GNB, *cf.* Myers). The two lists of eight Levites have five names in common, and each list has a further three of its own. Evidently, then, the two groups had different functions, partly glimpsed in 4b and 5b, where the first company seems to have voiced the distress of God's people (since the word for *cried* has this flavour), and the second led their corporate praise.

The call in verse 5b, *Stand up and bless the Lord*, and the blessing itself, continue to be heard today in the fine hymn by James Montgomery which opens with these words. The barely habitable city, the encircling heathen, and the poverty and seeming insignificance of the Jews are all transcended by the glorious reality of God. The facts are not ignored, as the ensuing prayer will show, but they will be seen in the context of eternity (*everlasting to everlasting*) and of God's unimaginable greatness (*above all blessing and praise*).

### 9:6-15. The Creator and Saviour

Verse 5b may well be the first sentence of this prayer, since the words *And Ezra said* (6a, RSV) are not in the Hebrew text. They are borrowed from LXX, and while they could be original, there is no compelling reason to accept them as such.[2]

The prayer is, like some of the Psalms (*e.g.* 78; 105; 106), an example of confession in both senses of the word: *i.e.*, a confessing of God's glory and grace as well as man's ingratitude. So it is worship, not mere wallowing in self-reproach. It shows, too, the influence of the scripture reading of the recent weeks, for it begins, like Genesis, at the creation (note the expression, *with all their host*, as in Gn. 2:1, Heb.), pauses on the re-naming and the faith of Abram (7f.) which no other Old Testament passage after Genesis picks out for mention, and notes not only God's covenant with him but the characteristic pentateuchal list of nations to be

[1] Middoth 2.5.
[2] There is some roughness of style, or else an error of copying, in the last sentence of 5b, which runs 'And let them bless thy glorious name . . .', which may indicate that the Levites at this point lifted their hands heavenwards, with a gesture that gathered up the congregation's response. GNB accordingly inserts (but without textual support) an explanatory opening to 6a: 'And then the people of Israel prayed this prayer'.

dispossessed, from Canaanites to Girgashites (8). Note too the unmistakable echo of the song at the Red Sea in the phrase *as a stone into mighty waters* (11; Ex. 15 : 5, 10).

So the theme of promise and fulfilment, stated in 8b, unfolds in the familiar events of the Exodus (9–15); and throughout verses 6–15 God is the subject of every sentence.

### 9:16-25. **The generous and patient God**

*They* will now alternate with *Thou* as the confession develops. Each of the two parties, God and man, stands out with special clarity against the background of the other. Sin abounds, grace superabounds. Israel opts for turning back to Egypt and for a new god; the Lord stands by His people, keeps His promises and meets their deepest (20) and most elementary needs (21).[1] Throughout this miraculous pilgrimage 'they lacked nothing' (21)—and appreciated nothing (17). This part of their history ends with an undeserved and unstinted inheritance, 'full of all good things' (25).

### 9:26-31. **The God who warns and disciplines**

The confession moves on to the Judges period (and beyond, since the *prophets* chiefly lived—and died, 26f.—in the monarchy) reproducing the rhythm of that era with its steady repetition of sin, decline, appeal and rescue, a cycle which no warnings from experience or from preaching could do anything to break. Here again the sharp contrast between man and God stands out, marked (for us[2]) by the words *Nevertheless they* . . . in the opening verse of the paragraph (26) and *Nevertheless . . . thou* at the close (31).

### 9:32-37. **The low ebb of God's people**

**32.** The string of divine epithets at the beginning of this verse, and of human office-bearers and others at its close, is not mere rhetoric. Troubles are put in perspective by the former, and human structures and resources into prominence by the latter. Just how shattering the loss of *kings . . . princes, etc.*, had seemed, can still be keenly felt through the agonized words of Lamentations 4 : 20; 5 : 12; 2 : 9, 20 . . ., and it would have been

---

[1] With verse 20 *cf.* Ex. 31 : 3; Nu. 11 : 17; 27 : 18ff.; Is. 63 : 10, 14. With verse 21 *cf.* Dt. 8 : 4.
[2] The Heb., however, has simply the conjunction which serves for 'and' or 'but' according to context.

unrealistic to deny it. But the words used of God point to far more solid realities, and each of them is distinctive. To take only the adjectives, *great* is a reminder that God does not share our narrowness of vision or of being; *mighty* is a virile word, fit to describe the paladins who did exploits for David (2 Sa. 23:8ff.), or 'the King of glory . . ., mighty in battle' (Ps. 24:8), or the divine prince of Isaiah 9:6. *Terrible* is misleading, for the word used here means awe-inspiring, not ruthless. It is related to the expression 'the fear of the Lord', that filial relationship which, in the most positive of senses, puts us securely in our place, and God in His (a theme thankfully developed in, *e.g.*, Ps. 34:7ff.).

*The kings of Assyria* were the first of the successive world powers to menace and then subjugate Israel and Judah since the bondage in Egypt. From the middle of the 9th century BC to Nehemiah's day in the middle of the 5th century, first Assyria, intermittently, then Babylon and now Persia had dominated this small people. And Greece and Rome were to follow.

**33-35.** There is all the difference here between self-pity and self-knowledge. The painful admission, *yet thou hast been just*, like that of the penitent thief, would open the door to mercy; and the sad catalogue of *kings, princes* and others lamented in verse 32 has become material for confession in verses 34f.

**36, 37.** Some writers have questioned whether Ezra or Nehemiah, as protégés of Artaxerxes, would have spoken in this fashion of the Persian power. Others, however, have recognized here the proper zeal for God and Israel which no amount of royal patronage had any right to compromise. This prayer is not breathing out rebellion, nor complaining of injustice (notice the phrase, *because of our sins*, 37, in line with 33ff.), but neither is it pretending that to serve and enrich a foreign régime is what was promised to Abraham and his seed. The *great distress* which ends the prayer is a sign of life and of a vision that has not been tamely given up.

### Nehemiah 9:38 - 10:39. The binding declaration

This chapter[1] clinches the confession just made. Those who prayed have asked for mercy but do not mean to trade on it, as their 'binding declaration' (9:38, NEB) makes clear.

---

[1] In the Heb. Bible, chapter 10 begins at our 9:38.

**9:38.** The term *covenant* is not in the text, which uses the word '*a̅ma̅na̅*, 'a firm (promise)' (*cf.* 11:23, and comment); but the verb translated 'make' is *ka̅rat*, 'to cut', which has strong associations with covenant-making. The three classes of signatories[1] will divide up the ensuing list of names, though the priests will precede the Levites there.

The inverted commas should not have been closed at 9:37, for this passage (including the list of names) is as definitely a 'we'-passage as the prayer which has led up to it.

### 10:1-27. The signatories

**1.** There is an 'and' (omitted in RSV) between Nehemiah and Zedekiah, but not between or before the names that follow in verses 2-8; which indicates that these first two are a group apart, evidently representing the civil power.

**2-8.** There are twenty-one priestly names here, of which at least fifteen are names of families. This is clear from chapter 12, whose list of the original homecomers from Babylon has many of the names found again here (Seraiah, Jeremiah, Amariah, *etc.*), and which goes on to mention separately the individuals who, at a certain period, were heads of these 'fathers' houses' (see on 12:1-7).[2] This accounts, incidentally, for the non-appearance of Ezra's name among the signatories, since he was a member of the family which heads the list, the house of *Seraiah* (which also included the high priest): *cf.* Ezra 7:1(-5) with 1 Chronicles 6:(3-)14.

**9-13.** Of these seventeen Levite names, some may indicate family groups of long standing (*e.g.*, the first three names coincide with those Levites in 12:8a who came home with Zerubbabel[3]), but several are of contemporary individuals. Six of them, possibly seven, were among the teaching group at Ezra's reading of the law (Ne. 8:7), and *Sherebiah* has met us not only there but (if it is the same man) as a prominent member of Ezra's original expedition (Ezr. 8:18). *Hashabiah* was with him (Ezr. 8:19), and was one of the builders of Nehemiah's wall (Ne. 3:17)—if, again, it is the same person in each context.

**14-27.** *The chiefs of the people* are listed predominantly

---

[1] The actual expression used in 9:38; 10:1 (10:1, 2, Heb.) is 'upon the sealed thing(s) are . . .' (our princes, *etc.*). *I.e.*, 'these names are hereby affixed'; or just possibly, 'the document was sealed under their inspection' (*cf.* NEB).

[2] *Cf.* also Ezr. 2:38 (Pashhur), 39 (Harim).

[3] *Cf.* also Ezr. 2:40 (the sons of Jeshua and Kadmiel).

(perhaps entirely) in terms of the families they represented; in fact the first twenty-one names (Parosh to Magpiash, 14-20a) closely follow the list in Ezra 2 : 3-30, with a few variants of order and spelling. Nehemiah, it will be remembered, had used that document in enrolling his community (Ne. 7 : 5). Some of the remaining twenty-three names, in 20-26, have also appeared as fathers' names, *i.e.*, family names, in the list of wall builders in Nehemiah 3.[1] Of the many new families since Zerubbabel's time (Ezr. 2), some will probably have arisen as branches of older ones, and others as more recent arrivals.

### 10:28, 29. The general oath of obedience

This picks up and fills out the declaration made in 9 : 38 by the whole company and sealed on their behalf by their leaders. It is made completely clear that everyone, down to the youngest children who could understand (28c; *cf.* 8 : 2 and comment), shared in this *oath* (reinforced by a *curse, i.e.*, by calling down disaster if they should go back on their word).

The list not only emphasizes this unanimity, but portrays the people as an ordered company, enrolled (7 : 5 again) in its traditional groups as exemplified in Ezra 2 : 36ff. (when the returned exiles had made a point of restoring the authentic life of Israel) and conscious of its calling to be *separated . . . from the peoples*. The reading of the law (*e.g.* Lv. 20 : 26) had left no room for doubt of this.

### 10:30-39. The particular pledges

The whole company had bowed to the whole law (29b), but there were parts of it which impinged on them with special force.

**30. Mixed marriages.** The law had strongly condemned these (not on racial but on religious grounds, Ex. 34 : 12-16; hence the ready acceptance of Ruth the convert). But the social climb was tempting in these trying days, and marriage offered an attractive ladder. Malachi (2 : 10-16), Ezra (9 : 1ff.) and Nehemiah (13 : 23-29) all encountered the problem, tackling it firmly in their different ways. Finally, lest the Christian should think it no longer a live issue, Paul expounds it with unanswerable logic and passionate intensity in 2 Corinthians 6 : 14 - 7 : 1.

[1] *E.g.*, Meshezabel, Baana, 3 : 4; Harim, 3 : 11; Hallohesh, 3 : 12. There are other names common to both contexts, but it must always be kept in mind that a name can belong to more than one person or family.

**31. The sabbath.** The presence of foreign traders opened a loophole in the sabbath law, for one could argue that no-one in the covenant was being put to any work in buying from them. But the people could now see that the tone and spirit of the day were being threatened. Later, when they went back on their decision, it was soon apparent how serious a threat it posed (see the vivid report in 13:15-22).

On the *seventh year*, see Exodus 23:11; Leviticus 25:4-7, 20-22 ('What shall we eat in the seventh year . . .?'); Deuteronomy 15:1-11.

**32, 33. Temple tax.** In Exodus 30:11-16 everyone over 20 was charged half a shekel as 'a ransom for himself', and this money was used 'for the service of the tent of meeting'. But it was levied only when a census was held, whereas the present passage promises a slightly smaller but annual sum. (In NT times it had become half a shekel: Mt. 17:24.) As Brockington points out, although the decrees of Cyrus, Darius and Artaxerxes authorized regular grants from public funds for the costs of worship (*e.g.* Ezr. 6:8-10), these could not be expected to continue indefinitely; nor (we may add) would such dependence on foreign patronage have been healthy for Judaism.

**34-39. Offerings in kind.** Some of the details are new; others reaffirm what is written in the law. Experience had evidently shown that 'what is everybody's business is nobody's business', hence the allotting of responsibility for firewood (34). It was also good administration to have it clearly understood that the Levites were authorized to collect the rural tithes (37b), and that they should not do it unsupervised (38a).

*The tithe of the tithes* (38), *i.e.*, a tenth of the tenths, refers to Numbers 18:26, in a passage which shows that the Levites, as recipients of the tithes of all Israel, had to tithe what they received and pass on this tenth share to the priests. In Moses' day, when Levites greatly outnumbered priests, this gave a reasonable proportion to both groups, but now it bore hardly on the priests. The fact that they nevertheless accepted the position shows how sacrosanct the law was to them. Some implications of this for pentateuchal criticism, pointed out by Y. Kaufmann, are discussed in the comment on Ezra 2:40-42.

The final pledge, *We will not neglect the house of our God* (39), sums up not only the paragraph but much of the concern of the post-exilic prophets, Haggai, Zechariah and Malachi. Before the exile, the Temple had too often been a mere talisman, and its well-patronized activities a sedative for the conscience (see, above all, Je. 7). Now the temptation was the opposite: to grudge the effort and expense of it all. The mood is captured and castigated in Malachi. The very different tone of this chapter is some measure of Ezra's and Nehemiah's leadership, and of the impact of the Word of God on those who were exposed to it at length and in depth. On this, see again 8 : 7f., 12f., 18; 9 : 3.

## Nehemiah 11. An ordered society

It is not bureaucratic pedantry that has preserved these names. The point is, once more, that these people and their chronicler are conscious of their roots and of their structure as God's company. This is no rabble of refugees, settling down anywhere: they have the dignity of order and of known relationships; above all, of their calling to be 'a kingdom of priests and a holy nation' (Ex. 19 : 6).

We learn from 1 Chronicles 9 : 3 (in a chapter which fills out the present list with further names and with glimpses of the Temple servants at their work) that Israelites of other tribes than the three mentioned here took up residence in Jerusalem. But these three, Judah, Benjamin and Levi, were the nucleus. These had stayed with David's heirs, to form the kingdom of Judah when the rest had broken away; now the future of Israel lay with them and with those who had rallied to them from the other tribes.

### 11 : 1-24. The peopling of Jerusalem
**1-3. The basic arrangement.** Jerusalem, as the capital and *the holy city* (1), was the obvious centre for the leaders and for most of the Temple staff; but it also needed other citizens to make it a balanced and defensible community. The rather bleak conditions are evident in 7 : 1-4. In the present chapter, verse 1a tells of a fresh move, not an existing situation, and is better translated by NEB, *etc.*, as 'The leaders of the people settled in Jerusalem'. Whether the volunteers of verse 2 were additional to the ones chosen by ballot, or whether the verse is saying that the latter accepted the decision cheerfully, we cannot be certain. But it was a promising start and another instance of the new eagerness to see Judah and Jerusalem restored to their proper glory.

Verse 3 shows that apart from the highest officials there was a fairly complete cross-section of the community, including priests, living in the other towns of Judah. The term, *Israel*, in this context, means ordinary citizens. On the last two categories of this verse, see on Ezra 2:43-58.

**4-6. Judahites in Jerusalem.** The list in 1 Chronicles 9:4-6 adds another branch of the tribe: the descendants of Zerah the twin brother of *Perez* (Gn. 38:27-30). The group headed by *Maaseiah* (5) was evidently descended from Judah's son Shelah (Gn. 38:5, 26), since *Shilonite* should almost certainly have the vowels of Shelanite (NEB; *cf.* GNB, JB) as in Numbers 26:20. *Valiant men* could be translated 'men of substance' (NEB), or 'outstanding men' (GNB), as it can denote wealth, strength or ability, and is not as closely tied to physical prowess as the expression in verse 14. Yet, since a major reason for populating Jerusalem was to defend it, 'valiant' is probably right.

**7-9. Benjaminites in Jerusalem.** The list in 1 Chronicles 9:7-9 is fuller and reaches a slightly larger total (956); it also mentions that the people in question were all 'heads of fathers' houses'. The mention of *their overseer* (9; *cf.* verses 14 and 22, and 12:42) makes it doubly clear that the population was not an amorphous mass but an ordered society, as befitted the people of 'the holy city' (1, 18). The office held by Judah the son of Hassenuah[1] is slightly puzzling, in view of Hananiah's appointment in 7:2, but Judah may have been in charge of the 'second quarter' of the city (NEB mg.; *cf.* 2 Ki. 22:14).

**10-14. The priests in Jerusalem.** We have already noticed (see on 10:2-8) that lists of this kind refer sometimes to families, not always naming (as 12:12ff. does) the current clan chief. This, together with the tendency of the priesthood to perpetuate a small stock of favourite names (*cf.* Lk. 1:61), makes this register difficult to interpret with any certainty.[2]

The expression, *who did the work of the house* (12), *i.e.* of the Temple, implies that some less ceremonial duties fell to other

[1] This name, if spelt with a different 's' (*s̆*), could mean 'the unloved (wife)'; *cf.* Gn. 29:31. But although the two kinds of 's' can change places, the variant form Hassenaah (Ne. 3:3) and the (?) town-name Senaah (Ezr. 2:35) should discourage etymological speculation such as BDB's 'the poorer classes' (after E. Meyer).

[2] There is also some textual uncertainty in verse 10, where *ben* (*the son of*) should perhaps be omitted. It is absent from the parallel verse 1 Ch. 9:10, in which Jehoiarib, Jedaiah and Jachin are heads of three, not two, priestly houses, as also in 1 Ch. 24:7, 17. But there is no textual basis for the emendation in JB, NEB, which omits Jachin (*ykyn*) as a presumed miscopying of *ben*, 'son of' (*bn*), and makes the whole list of names a genealogy for Jedaiah.

groups. One such task was that of teaching (Mal. 2:7); another for the time being, in the precarious state of Jerusalem (*cf.* Ne. 7:3f.), may well have been defence. *Mighty men of valour* (14) is normally a military epithet, stronger than that of verse 6. Although in Ruth 2:1 it is used of Boaz as a man of wealth or ability, here it most probably has its familiar meaning of physical prowess.

The word *Haggedolim* is a plural form ('the great'), and slightly unusual as a personal name. GNB may be right in taking it to mean 'a leading family'.

**15-24. Levites and Temple staff in Jerusalem.** The glimpses of the people involved in Temple duties are tantalizingly brief, but enough to indicate the hive of activity that was maintained there. The picture comes to life more fully in 1 Chronicles 9:17-34, where we see the posting of the gatekeepers, the checking in and out of utensils, the preparing of offering-cakes, and so on. Here the mention of *the outside work* (16) tells its tale of the supplies and maintenance that a large establishment requires, while the next verse recalls us to the point of it all, *the thanksgiving in prayer* (17).[1] The names *Asaph* and *Jeduthun* in this verse go back to David's founding of the Temple choirs and bands (2 Ch. 5:12). There is more about the singers in verses 22-24.

**18.** Notice again the significant expression, *the holy city*, as in verse 1. It was a name to live up to. The number given for all the Levites may include the 172 gatekeepers mentioned in the next verse, since these also belonged to Levi (Ezr. 2:40-42). On the other hand, 'Levites' in the present verse may be used in its narrower sense of assistants to the priests.

**19, 20.** The duties of these gatekeeper families (more of whom are named in 12:25) are explained more fully in 1 Chronicles 9:17-27, where it appears that the security of the Temple area was their hereditary charge, and that their number was supplemented by non-resident kinsmen (hence, no doubt, the larger total in 1 Ch. 9:22) who came in from their villages for a week's duty at a time. The Temple needed a strong guard on account of both its treasures and its sacredness. The questions and answers in, *e.g.*, Psalms 15 and 24 about ascending the hill of

---

[1] The Heb. is awkward at this point, though the general sense is fairly clear. It runs: '. . . the head of the beginning, (who) gave thanks at the prayer.' Possibly 'beginning' (*t⁽ᵉ⁾ḥillâ*) should be 'praise' (*t⁽ᵉ⁾ḥillâ*), as Vulg. reads it; but as Ryle points out, the obscure phraseology may preserve technical terms used in the choir.

the Lord, and the brief exchange in Psalm 118:19f., may be echoes of the kind of challenge that these guardians of the sanctuary would put to those who sought entry. Incidentally the famous line in Psalm 84:10, 'I would rather be a doorkeeper...', does not refer to these honoured officials but rather, it seems, to the worshipper on the very outskirts of the crowd, who has ventured no further than the threshold.

**21.** On the *temple servants*, or Nethinim (RV), see on Ezra 2:43. They, unlike the groups mentioned in verse 20, had no non-resident colleagues. *Ophel* (*cf.* 3:26) was the hill leading up to the Temple at the north end of the city.

**22, 23.** In contrast, it seems, to the officials who supervised the 'outside work' (see on verse 16), the Asaphite *Uzzi*[1] was responsible for what is simply called *the work of the house of God*, which the context implies to be the choral worship. The RSV of verse 23 (following AV, RV; but see AV mg., RV mg.) sees in this *a settled provision for the singers*, by royal command; but 'settled provision' is a single Hebrew word ($^{a}m\bar{a}n\hat{a}$) for something sure or firm, and more likely to mean 'regulations' (JB, GNB; *cf.* NEB).[2] The expression *as every day required* is literally 'a day's matter on its day', and the verse is probably concerned with the service times of the choirs, for which the 'overseer' of verse 22 was responsible. Worship was too important to be left unplanned.

**24.** The mention of the king in verse 23 is now clarified: at court he had his commissioners from the subject peoples to advise on their affairs. There is a Pethahiah mentioned in Ezra 10:23, and a Meshezabel in Nehemiah 3:4.

## 11:25-36. The villages of Judah and Benjamin

As a province of the Persian empire, the whole territory governed by Nehemiah was called Yehud (Judah), and was bounded on the north by the province of Samaria, and on the south by Idumea (Edom). But historically the part of it which ran from Jerusalem northward had belonged to Benjamin; so the

[1] As the great-grandson of Mattaniah-ben-Mica he seems at first sight an unlikely contemporary of the Mattaniah-ben-Mica of verse 17. But as Brockington points out, the latter could well have been named after the common great-grandfather, since 'papponymy' (the naming of children after their grandfathers) was increasingly the fashion in post-exilic Judaism. See also on verse 10, and note too the repeated sequence Amariah-Ahitub-Zadok in 1 Ch. 6:7f. and 11f.

[2] Its only other occurrence is in 9:38 (10:1, Heb.), where it is translated 'a firm covenant'.

two tribes occupied their respective territories, defined briefly in verses 30b, 31a, with Levi distributed among them both (36); also (as we learn from elsewhere, *e.g.* 1 Ch. 9:3) with certain survivors of the northern tribes.

What is surprising at first sight is that this re-settlement goes beyond the confines of the new, small province, to include places that had belonged to Judah in the old days. *Kiriath-arba* (25), *i.e.* Hebron (Jos. 14:15), twenty miles south of Jerusalem, was almost certainly within Idumea, and there is no doubt about *Beer-sheba* (27), at twice the distance. But as citizens of the one empire, these people were free to settle where they would, provided they kept the peace; therefore what is shown here is a return of families to their native parts wherever possible, not an attempted expansion of the province. Possibly the expression, *so they encamped* (30), reflects this sense of being present somewhat on sufferance, even in their own land—a sense which found words in the *cri de coeur* of 9:36f.

Among the place-names, we may note briefly *Dibon* (25), distinct from the Moabite Dibon of Isaiah 15:9; *the valley of Hinnom* (30), outside the south wall of Jerusalem, recorded as a boundary of Judah in Joshua 15:8; *Hazor* (33), not to be confused with Jabin's northern stronghold (there are several Hazors in the OT); *Ono* (35): see on 6:2. Brockington suggests that the *craftsmen* of that district may have been workers in wood, since it was not far from Joppa, the unloading-point for timber from Lebanon (Ezr. 3:7).

## Nehemiah 12:1–26. Registers of priests and Levites

Continuity is again a major interest here. Unexciting as the first half of the chapter is, it has a point to make by its refusal to treat bygone generations as of no further interest. And if history-writing inevitably distorts reality by its concentration on outstanding people and on the forces of change, here is something to redress the balance.

**1–7. Priestly houses at the return from exile.** There are twenty-two names here, and it becomes clear from verses 12–21 that the priestly houses continued to be known by reference to them—indeed fifteen of Nehemiah's contemporaries sealed the 'firm covenant' of chapter 10 with these family names (see the list below), while only a small minority appear to have used their personal names.

Since there were originally twenty-four priestly divisions for sanctuary duties (1 Ch. 24:7-19), and this number was in force again in later Judaism, it may be that two names have dropped out in the copying, just as one name in the present list (Hattush, verse 2) has failed to reappear in verses 12-21. But equally it may be that the full rota had not yet been restored.

For comparison, these are the houses named at three points in the book:

| Nehemiah 12:1-7 (the first homecomers) | Nehemiah 12:12-21 (the, or a, subsequent generation) | Nehemiah 10:2-8 (Nehemiah's generation) |
|---|---|---|
| Seraiah | Seraiah | Seraiah |
| Jeremiah | Jeremiah | Azariah |
| Ezra | Ezra | Jeremiah |
| Amariah | Amariah | Pashhur* |
| Malluch | Malluchi | Amariah |
| Hattush | Shebaniah | Malchijah* |
| Shecaniah | Harim | Hattush |
| Rehum | Meraioth | Shebaniah |
| Meremoth | Iddo | Malluch |
| Iddo | Ginnethon | Harim |
| Ginnethoi | Abijah | Meremoth |
| Abijah | Miniamin | Obadiah* |
| Mijamin | Moadiah | Daniel* |
| Maadiah | Bilgah | Ginnethon |
| Bilgah | Shemaiah | Baruch* |
| Shemaiah | Joiarib | Meshullam* |
| Joiarib | Jedaiah | Abijah |
| Jedaiah | Sallai | Mijamin |
| Sallu | Amok | Maaziah |
| Amok | Hilkiah | Bilgai |
| Hilkiah | Jedaiah | Shemaiah |
| Jedaiah | | * names confined to this list. |

Among the spelling variations, the name Azariah (second in the right-hand column) should probably be included, being a longer form of the name Ezra ('help'): *i.e.*, 'Yahweh has helped'. Another of the less obvious variations is probably Rehum (12:3) for Harim (12:15; 10:5), representing a transposition of the first two consonants, since vowels were not part of the original text.

**8, 9. Levitical families at the return from exile.** This fills out the summary given in Ezra 2:40f., which has only the family names Jeshua, Kadmiel, Hodaviah and (of the singers) Asaph. Probably Judah in our passage is the same as the Hodaviah of Ezra 2:40 with 3:9 (from the same Heb. root); and Binnui may link up with Ezra 3:9 in the light of Nehemiah 3:24. Other names in the list (*e.g.* Sherebiah; *cf.* 8:7; 9:4; 10:12) were treasured enough to be still used as levitical names in Nehemiah's day, attached in some cases to the same office as at the first. So Mattaniah and Bakbukiah, leaders of the antiphonal singing at the time of the return, are the names we encounter in identical roles in 11:17 where the scene is a century later, and again in 12:25 where the continuity with David's original régime is emphasized.[1]

**10, 11. The high-priestly family.** This bridges the gap between the first generation after the exile (the period of verses 1-9) and the contemporaries of Nehemiah. It carries forward the genealogy of 1 Chronicles 6:3-15, which ran from Aaron to the Babylonian exile; and like that document, which omits some names known to us from other scriptures, it does not necessarily include every generation. Between Jeshua, who returned from Babylon in 538, and Eliashib, the high priest in Nehemiah's time about a century later, Joiakim (10) may not have been the only link in the chain, though it is not impossible that he was.

The names Jonathan and Jaddua here (11), and Darius and Johanan in verses 22f., raise some historical questions which are discussed in Appendix III, pp. 144f. Briefly, the point at issue is whether the list takes us to the end of the Persian period, about a hundred years after Nehemiah, in the reign of Darius III (336/5-331), or whether it takes us only as far as Darius II (423-404), the king who followed Nehemiah's patron Artaxerxes I. It hinges on the reliance to be placed on Josephus's chronology and on the very doubtful legitimacy of identifying, *e.g.*, Jonathan-ben-Joiada (11) with Johanan-ben-Eliashib (23), and equating certain names mentioned by Josephus with similar names from another source, the Elephantine papyri. As Appendix III argues, it seems safest to conclude that the lists here

---

[1] The name Bukkiah (1 Ch. 25:4), listed with Mattaniah among David's musicians, is probably the prototype of the form Bakbukiah. Unni (*cf.* Unno, verse 9) is another such name in 1 Ch. 15:20. And Abda (Ne. 11:17) is a shortened form of Obadiah, a name listed with Mattaniah and Bakbukiah in 12:25.

go no further than Darius II (*i.e.*, Nehemiah's lifetime, or soon after) and that Josephus's account of the murderous high priest Joannes and of Jaddua his son refers not to the people named in verses 11 and 22f. but to their successors of a generation or two later See also on 13:28f.

**12-21. Heads of priestly families in the second generation.** Joiakim (12) was the son of Jeshua, who was high priest at the time of the return from Babylon. (On the apparently long span of Joiakim's career see on verses 10f., above.) As we have already noticed, in the comments on verses 1-7, the particular interest of this paragraph lies in its clear evidence that the priestly houses held on to their traditional names, not changing them with successive leaders.

**22-26. Heads of levitical families.** Before the monarchy successive eras were reckoned by the lifetimes of the high priests (*cf.* Nu. 35:28), and now again, in the absence of a king, theirs are the names which mark the times.

**22.** Eliashib was the high priest in office at Nehemiah's arrival in Jerusalem (3:1). Johanan is described as his son[1] (23); therefore (if 'son' is meant literally) he appears to have followed his brother Joiada in the high priesthood. This is discussed further in Appendix IV, p. 154. From the Elephantine papyri (see Appendix III, p. 143) it is known that the high priest in 410 BC, in the reign of Darius II,[2] was named Johanan. The name and date fit in well with our passage.

**23.** *The Book of the Chronicles* ('the book of day-to-day events') was the record book, not the biblical 1 and 2 Chronicles. On Johanan, see verse 22 and footnote to it.

**24, 25.** The names in verse 24 have come also in the list of Levites who set their seal to the declaration in chapter 10, and most of them have recurred in the present chapter, verse 8. In

---

[1] JB, NEB, GNB, however, assume that Jonathan (11) and Johanan (23) were the same person, and translate 'son' as 'grandson'. Although this extended meaning is possible, its adoption here begs an important chronological question, which is discussed in Appendix IV, p. 154. GNB alone takes the further and unjustifiable step of substituting the name Jonathan for Johanan here, without comment.

[2] The phrase, *until the reign* (22, RSV), is an emendation. The MT, supported by the ancient versions, has the preposition '*al* ('on'; possibly 'in connection with', *cf.* BDB 754e), hence RV 'in the reign'. This seems to imply that the priests were recorded for a more limited period than the Levites, which is unlikely. The simplest conjecture is an early scribal error ('*al* for '*ad*, as in verse 23, 'until'), before the compiling of LXX. On the question, Darius II or III, see on verses 10, 11, above, or Appendix III, pp. 144ff.

verse 24 there is almost certainly a scribal error between the names Jeshua and Kadmiel, where 'the son of' (Heb. *ben*) should read, instead, 'Binnui' as in verse 8; *cf.* 10:9.

In David's system the phrase, *watch corresponding to watch*, applied to the gatekeepers (1 Ch. 26:16). Here it seems to govern primarily the singers, who are also shown standing opposite one another, both earlier in this verse and in verse 9. But verse 25 seems to make the first three names both singers (see on verses 8, 9) and gatekeepers, unless we reckon that verse 24 should continue as far as the name Obadiah in its list of singers, and verse 25 begin with Meshullam.[1]

**26.** This stresses, once more, the continuity of family responsibilities for Temple service, spanning the best part of a century. The various chronological notes, chiefly introduced by the phrase, *in the days of . . . (cf.* verses 7, 12, 22, 23), are not always easy to relate to one another, but the difficulties arise chiefly from the multiplicity of lists used by the compiler. In passing, we may note that the Hebrew of this verse couples Nehemiah and Ezra more closely than do most of our translations, which should omit the word *'of'* before Ezra's name.[2]

### Nehemiah 12:27-43. The wall is dedicated

At this point, or else at verse 31, we are back with the first-person memoirs of Nehemiah. His voice was last heard directly at 7:5, where he introduced the list of the first homecomers; after that, the editor took up the narrative, speaking of Nehemiah in the third person (8:9; 10:1; 12:26).

**27-30. Preparations for the day.** Elaborate festivities can be hollow, but where the occasion is great, the demanding business of planning, proclaiming, assembling[3] and rehearsing makes good kindling material for the emotions; not a substitute

[1] On Obadiah, see the footnote to verses 8, 9. Meshullam may be a variant of the name Shallum, found in the list of gatekeeper families in Ezr. 2:42, along with Talmon, Akkub and others.

[2] On the intention of the text to present the two men as contemporaries, with Nehemiah the senior in rank, see Rudolph, p. 195. *Cf.* W. Th. In der Smitten, *Esra: Quellen, Überlieferung und Geschichte* (Van Gorcum, 1973), pp. 95f. GNB, lapsing from impartiality, inserts 'the time of' at this point, evidently under the influence of the theory that the two men were not contemporaries.

[3] Points mentioned here from 'the circuit round Jerusalem' are to the south (Netophah, in Judah, Ezr. 2:22), the east (if Beth-gilgal is the same as Gilgal, Jos. 4:19) and the north (Geba and Azmaveth in Benjamin).

for the more searching preparations seen in verse 30 (where nobody and nothing was left unpurified), but not by any means to be despised. If the New Testament emphasizes what is inward and spiritual in worship, it has a place too for the natural means of encouraging and stirring us. Our Lord went to Gethsemane fortified not only by prayer but by a ceremonial meal and corporate singing, matters which engage not only the spirit but the body and the senses.

**31–43. The twin processions.** There was much more than pageantry in this processional embrace of the city and its walls. It was an extended thanksgiving and a re-consecration, a claiming of these stones for Israel and for God; and if, as seems likely, it took place before the events of chapter 11, it gives added point to the expression there, 'the holy city' (11:1, 18). But we should misunderstand this if we thought of it as the drawing of a sacred circle in some semi-magical sense, for its dominant note was confession of what God had done (see on verse 31). Psalm 48 describes a somewhat similar beating of the bounds, and lays its emphasis on what this act should do for the worshippers, not for the battlements, by its tangible reminder of God's providence:

> 'Make the round of Zion in procession,
>   count the number of her towers,
> take good note of her ramparts,
>   pass her palaces in review,
> that you may tell generations yet to come:
>   Such is God,
> our God for ever and ever;
>   he shall be our guide eternally.'
>                           (Ps. 48:12-14, NEB)

Strikingly enough, the expression, the *companies which gave thanks* (31), and the similar phrases in verses 38 and 40, translate a single Hebrew word *tôdōt*, 'thanksgivings' or 'confessions'—almost as though these choirs were the embodiment of what they sang. So one 'thanksgiving'went to the right (31), the other to the left (38), and eventually both 'thanksgivings' stood in the house of God (40).

Not knowing their starting-point, we cannot be quite certain of their routes, but the first paragraph is so reminiscent of Nehemiah's nocturnal reconnaissance in 2:12ff. that we may guess that, like him, they started from the Valley Gate on (it seems) the west side, Ezra's procession (36c) going anti-clockwise

along the southern and then the eastern wall[1] (*cf.* 31c and 37 with chapters 2:13f. and 3:13-26) towards the Temple, while Nehemiah's company (38) went the other way, towards and along the north wall. Some of the landmarks of verses 38f. were mentioned in 3:1-11 and 28-32, in the account of the repair work. Every inch of these ramparts had its special memory for one group or another.

Nevertheless, the destination was *the house of God* (40), for the walls were, appropriately, the circumference not the focal point of the celebrations, and it was the choirs, not the officials, who led the way. So while *Ezra the scribe* (36) headed the first procession, Nehemiah's place in the other group was after the choir (38);[2] and the climax was the offering of *great sacrifices . . . with great joy* (43). This time, in contrast to Ezra 3:13, it was no uncertain sound that was heard afar off.

## Nehemiah 12:44 – 13:3. 'Decently and in order'

### 12:44-47. The sinews of worship

It is one thing to shout on a great occasion, but another to offer the sacrifice of praise continually and to make realistic provision for the church's needs. The expression, *On that day* (44), suggests that no time was lost in attending to this; and it would be typical of Nehemiah to strike while the iron was hot, gaining something practical from this moment of elation and goodwill—for Judah's enthusiasm over the clergy (44c) was nothing to be counted on, as 13:10ff. would show.

Yet in 13:1 the same phrase, 'On that day', must be taken quite generally ('At that time', JB), since 13:4, 6 imply the passage of several years 'before this'. So GNB is probably right to

[1] 'Right' (31) and 'left' (38) are thus relative to one who is facing the west wall from outside, or who is standing on the wall and surveying the city from this point.
[2] Myers points out the symmetry of the arrangements, which he sets out somewhat as follows (abbreviated and slightly modified here):

| *Group led by Ezra, toward the right:* | *Group proceeding to the left:* |
| --- | --- |
| Thanksgiving choir | Thanksgiving choir |
| Hoshaiah | Nehemiah |
| 'Half of the princes' (v. 32) | 'Half of the officials' (v. 40) |
| Priests with trumpets | Priests with trumpets |
| (seven of them named, | (seven named, from |
| Azariah to Jeremiah) | Eliakim to Hananiah) |
| Instrumentalists | Singers |
| (Zechariah and eight others) | (Jezrabiah and eight others) |

have 'At that time' here. These two paragraphs, 12:44–47 and 13:1–3, are a historical aside, dropped in between two passages of Nehemiah's first-person memoirs.

**45, 46.** The mention of *David* and *Solomon* distinguishes the guilds of singers and gatekeepers, founded when Jerusalem became the settled place of worship,[1] from the priests and other Levites who served at the altar (45a). *Asaph* meets us chiefly in 1 Chronicles 15, 16 and 25 and in the titles of Psalms 50 and 73–83.

**47.** *The daily portions* translates the same striking Hebrew expression ('a day's matter on its day') as that of 11:23, rendered there by 'as every day required'. There, it probably referred to the day's duties (see the comment at that point), but here, to the day's supplies. The Christian can reflect that his Provider has a better memory than the men of Judah (see again 13:10).

On the 'tithe of the tithes' which was the priests' allowance, and on its implications, see on Ezra 2:40–42.

**13:1–3. A people apart**

We can identify the passage *from the book of Moses*, since verses 1 and 2 faithfully summarize Deuteronomy 23:3–5. True to the Old Testament's style, the prohibition is stark and unqualified, to make the most powerful impact, but the reader knows that elsewhere there are balancing considerations. It is the Ammonite or Moabite in his native capacity as the embodiment of Israel's inveterate enemy and corrupter who is in view: the son or 'daughter of a foreign god' (Mal. 2:11), burrowing into the life and even the language of Israel (verses 23ff.). But let him come as a convert, like Ruth the Moabitess, and he will be entitled to a very different reception.

Once again it was the public reading of Scripture which brought home to Israel its obligations as a people for God (*cf.* 8:1ff., 13ff.; 9:3ff.). Just when this reading took place is uncertain, since the expression, *On that day*, is not necessarily precise, and verses 4–6 show that it was after Nehemiah's first term of office as governor (see the second paragraph of comments on 12:44–47, above).

## Nehemiah 13:4–31. Nehemiah comes back

Once again, after the editorial interlude of 12:44 - 13:3,

[1] 1 Ch. 23:24ff.

Nehemiah speaks in the first person, in as hard-hitting and colourful a passage as any in the book. After twelve years as governor (445-433) he had returned to the emperor; then 'after some time' (verse 6) he obtained permission to go back to Jerusalem. If on his first visit he had been a whirlwind, on his second he was all fire and earthquake to a city that had settled down in his absence to a comfortable compromise with the gentile world.

### 13:4-9. Tobiah's furniture

Nehemiah's old enemy had always had admirers and sworn supporters in the highest circles of Judah (6:17-19). Himself the bearer of a good Jewish name (see on 2:10), he had married into one of the leading families, and his son into another, as reported earlier;[1] now it emerges that the high priest himself was a connection.[2]

Tobiah never lacked audacity. Where even a toe-hold in the temple would have been a conquest, he obtains a room the size of a small warehouse, and has it cleared for him by the religious authorities themselves (7). It was doubtless a special satisfaction to see his personal belongings take precedence over the very frankincense for God and the tithes for His ministers; but best of all he was at the nerve-centre of Jerusalem, ideally placed for influence and intrigue.

Unlike the ecclesiastics of the time who could see all sides of a matter, including the side to support, Nehemiah stormed in as violently as, one day, his Master would. Throughout this chapter he stands out from his contemporaries by his refusal to allow for a moment that holiness is negotiable or that custom alone can hallow anything.

For the chronology of this incident see verse 6, with 5:14 and the opening comments on 13:4-31, above.

### 13:10-14. A run-down establishment

A grudging attitude to tithes and offerings was a mark of the

---

[1] *Cf.* 6:18 with Ezr. 2:5 and Ne. 3:30.
[2] *Connected with* is lit. 'close to', which could mean 'hand in glove with' (*cf.* GNB) but is also a term for a family link. Some have questioned whether this *Eliashib* was the high priest, since the appointment 'over the chambers of the house' may seem a comparatively minor office. But a high official tends to have many such powers, and the point here is the abuse of the relevant one. Verse 28 shows the high priest's family in a similar entanglement to this one.

times. Before the exile, superstition had made people lavish with their religious gifts (*cf.* Am. 4: 4f.; 5: 22), but now the temptation was to give as little as one could—no longer out to bribe God but (in Malachi's expression) to 'rob' Him by defaulting. Nehemiah, faced now with the Levites' desertion of their posts, had the insight to put the blame where it belonged: not on the absentees of verse 10 but on the officials of verse 11. There had been great resolves of good stewardship in the 'firm covenant' of chapter 10, promising that 'We will not neglect the house of our God' (10: 39); but by now the fine words were feeding nobody. Nehemiah's own remonstrance would have achieved just as little, had he not followed it with the good administration of 11b and the careful appointments of verse 13.

**14.** To read such an interjection (see its companions in 5: 19 and verses 22, 29 and 31 of the present chapter) is almost to find oneself an eavesdropper. The memoirs become a personal outpouring, and we are intruders. But Nehemiah's private self is completely of a piece with his public one: singleminded, utterly frank, and godly through and through. If we cavil at his plea to be remembered, he could pronounce us too sophisticated; and the Gospels would support him. It springs from love, not self-love, as his tireless zeal for God has testified. To hear God's 'Well done' is the most innocent and most cleansing of ambitions. Further, the plea springs from humility, not self-importance, for it is an appeal for help. God's 'remembering' always implies His intervention, not merely His recollection or recognition. Nehemiah is committing himself and his cause (*cf.* 29) to the only safe hands. Incidentally *my good deeds* could be rendered 'my acts of loyal love', *i.e.*, of *ḥeseḏ*, which Brockington admirably defines here as 'that quality which will accept an obligation and honour it, come what may'. In verse 22 it is God who shows this quality ('steadfast love').

### 13:15-22. A threat to the sabbath

Before the exile there was a growing impatience with the sabbath law. Amos in the 8th century BC could see the merchants chafing at the weekly shut-down of business (Am. 8: 5); and sure enough, by Jeremiah's time they had had their way. Load after load of merchandise poured in and out of the city on the sabbath. Jeremiah's warning of what must follow (Je. 17: 19-27) was clearly in Nehemiah's mind as he saw the forbidden *burdens*[1] in

[1] The condemnation of the healed man in Jn. 5: 10 for carrying his pallet

transit (15; *cf.* Je. 17:21, *etc.*) and spoke of history repeating itself (18). The bustling scene of verses 15 and 16 shows how rapidly the trickle which must have begun in Nehemiah's absence (*cf.* verse 6 had become—as such trickles do—a flood.

**19ff.** Once more, remonstrance is reinforced with shrewd precautions, and precautions with alertness and pugnacity. Not even hucksters can steal a march on one so dedicated. And Nehemiah has the wisdom to hand on this charge to those who should keep it, making sure that they accept it as a holy task (*that they should purify themselves and come and guard the gates*, 22).

*Remember this also* ... (22): see on verse 14.

### 13:23-27. A threat to solidarity

'Ephraim', said Hosea (7:8f.), 'mixes himself with the peoples; ... Aliens devour his strength, and he knows it not.' Much is made in the Old Testament of the immediate disloyalties inherent in mixed marriages, but Nehemiah was struck by another aspect, barely touched on in the law or the prophets (except in the words 'Godly offspring', Mal. 2:15), namely the corruption of the *next* generation. The babble of languages among the children (24) was not only a symptom but a threat: it meant a steady erosion of Israelite identity at the level of all thinking and expression, and a loss of access to the Word of God, which would effectively paganize them. A single generation's compromise could undo the work of centuries.

Nehemiah's explosion was as characteristic as Ezra's *im*plosion had been. Both were powerfully effective, and both were to find some parallel in our Lord's encounters with evil. The shock treatment by Nehemiah was devastating in the same manner as the assault on the moneychangers, and the display of grief by Ezra (Ezr. 9:3ff.; 10:1ff.) was as moving, in its way, as the lament over Jerusalem.

Much has been deduced from the fact that Nehemiah made no use of the divorce procedure set up by Ezra, only taking steps to halt the spread or further outbreak of the trouble. This is discussed in Appendix IV, pp. 152f., where I argue that the reason lies in Nehemiah's preference for immediate and personal action, reinforced quite possibly by observation of the effects of the break-up of families under the previous régime (Ezr.

---

missed the point of Jeremiah's prohibition and equally of our Lord's command.

10:18-44)—rather than in any inversion, by the narrator, of the true sequence of events.

The measures of verse 25 were not simply an angry man's blind reactions. *I contended* uses the same verb as 'I remonstrated' in verses 11 and 17, *i.e.*, the word for arguing one's case against an opponent (arguments from history and from a stronger instance are used in verse 26). The rest of Nehemiah's onslaught used the leverage of divine sanctions (the curse; the promise under oath), physical pain, shame (*cf.* 2 Sa. 10:5; Is. 50:6 with the plucking of the hair) and an appeal to loyalty (27). It was a fearsome attack, but a crucial issue.

### 13:28, 29. A threat to the priesthood

Earlier in the chapter (verses 4ff.) the family link and close friendship between Eliashib and the notorious Tobiah had come to light. Sanballat ranked higher in the circle of Nehemiah's ill-wishers, and now with a daughter in the high priest's[1] family he had penetrated even further than his ally. It was a thrust almost to the heart. Nothing but a marriage to the high priest himself could have been more defiling. Whether Sanballat's daughter was legally disqualified by Leviticus 21:7 or not, the foothold which her father gained through her in the family made Jehoiada's consent to the marriage indefensible. By 'chasing' (glorious word!) her husband from the scene, Nehemiah effectively dislodged also both Sanballat and his daughter, and brought his own series of robust interventions to a fitting climax.[2]

### 13:30, 31. Epilogue

It may well reflect Nehemiah's scale of values that, while we

[1] The Heb. of verse 28 is ambiguous on the question whether 'high priest' refers to Jehoiada or to Eliashib. Jehoiada might well have succeeded to the office by this time.

[2] Josephus (*Ant.* xi. 7. 2) speaks of a Sanballat of Samaria, an official of Darius III (a century after the usual dating of Nehemiah), who married his daughter Nicaso to Manasseh, a brother of Jaddua the high priest. Manasseh, according to Josephus, avenged his expulsion by building the rival temple on Mt Gerizim, thereby founding the Samaritan sect. It is now generally agreed, however, that Josephus preserves 'a garbled version' (Coggins) of Nehemiah's story, his confusion partly arising out of the fact that two or perhaps three of the governors of Samaria in the century from Nehemiah to Darius III bore the name Sanballat (as the Samaria papyri from Waḍi Daliyeh indicate), and that there was apparently more than one Jaddua in the high-priestly family. See on 12:10, 11; also Appendix III, p. 145. The Samaria papyri are discussed by F. M. Cross in *BA* 26, pp. 110-121.

remember him for his city walls,[1] he ends his memoirs with a trio of achievements which are considerably less spectacular. The present chapter has exemplified the first two of them (filled out by chapters 10 to 12), and the items of verse 31 look back to 10:34f. This man from the imperial court brought no worldly values with him.

*I cleansed ... I established ... I provided*[2] *...* makes a far less brilliant epitaph than Caesar's boast, 'I came, I saw, I conquered.' But Nehemiah's work was the making of his people. His reforming zeal, partnered by the educative thoroughness of Ezra, gave to post-exilic Israel a virility and clarity of faith which it never wholly lost. This would have been the memorial most to his liking. This, indeed, now crowned by the lasting benefits of his book to the Christian church, surely constitutes a major part of heaven's answer to his repeated prayer (on which, see again on verse 14): *Remember me, O my God, for good.*

---

[1] Ecclus. 49:13 adds to this his rebuilding of houses.
[2] This verb is not part of the Heb. text, in which 'the wood offering', *etc.*, are additional objects of the verb 'I established'.

# APPENDICES

## a. Designations commonly in use

In the Hebrew Bible our two books are treated in some respects
as one, with a single massoretic paragraph-count for the two of
them at the end of Nehemiah. There is evidence that in early
Judaism they were collectively called Ezra.[1] This is also the case
in the Septuagint and Vulgate, but the matter is further
complicated by the existence of two apocryphal books of that
name (and by variations in the titles used in different versions
and editions). The following table, which is largely indebted to a
synopsis in Myers, may be useful for reference, but it by no means
exhausts the permutations.

| English | Septuagint | Vulgate |
|---|---|---|
| Ezra | Esdras B (or B 1–10) | Esdras I |
| Nehemiah | Esdras C (or B 11–23) | Esdras II |
| 1 Esdras (Apocrypha) | Esdras A | Esdras III |
| 2 Esdras (Apocrypha) | ——— | Esdras IV |

Of the two apocryphal books, 1 Esdras is a fragment consisting of
a parallel to 2 Chronicles 35:1 to Ezra 10 plus Nehemiah
8:1–13a and, at an earlier point, a speech-contest story (see
pp. 140f.). It is written in Greek. 2 Esdras is an apocalypse of
probably the late first century AD, whose Hebrew or Aramaic
original and Greek translation have perished, apart from a few
verses of the latter. Its Latin and other versions appear to be
secondary translations derived from the Greek.

## b. The sources

There is every sign of careful history-writing in our two canonical
books, in that almost the whole of the material is drawn from
primary sources.[2] These are of various kinds:

  1. *The memoirs of Ezra* (Ezr. 7:27 – 8:34 and the whole of

---

[1] *Talmud*: Nezikin, Baba Bathra 15a.
[2] Contrary opinions are discussed on pp. 165ff.

chapter 9). These are a first-person record of Ezra's expedition to Jerusalem and his reaction to the laxity that he found there.

2. *The memoirs of Nehemiah* (Ne. 1 and 2; 4:1 - 7:5; 12:(27 or) 31 - 43; 13:4 - end). This account, which is extremely outspoken, occupies about half the book.

3. *Jewish lists.* Some of these are evidently copied from Temple archives, others from the lay administration. The importance attached to such records can be seen from Ezra 2:59, 62. They included inventories (Ezr. 1:9ff.; 8:24-34; note verse 34), genealogies (Ezr. 2 = Ne. 7:6ff.; Ne. 12:1-26), the list of builders and their assignments (Ne. 3), a register of families and of categories of Temple officials resident in Jerusalem (Ne. 11:1-24), and a list of principal towns and villages assigned to Judah and Benjamin (Ne. 11:25-36). There were records of sacrifices (Ezr. 8:35f.; *cf.* 7:17, 22); there was also a name-list from the divorce court set up by Ezra (Ezr. 10:16-44), and a copy of the 'firm covenant' of Nehemiah 10, together with its list of signatories.

4. *Imperial decrees and correspondence.* Ancient administrators were as careful as their modern counterparts to keep records of decisions and letters, and there is direct evidence (Ne. 11:24) as well as indirect for the fact that the Persians used native advisers for the drafting of local regulations. Evidently our author had access to the archives (note the words, 'The copy of the letter . . .', in Ezr. 5:6; 7:11), and he allows them to speak for themselves, giving us not only, for instance, the proclamation of Cyrus intended for public consumption (Ezr. 1:2-4), but the minute which supplied the administrative details (Ezr. 6:1-5). Exchanges of correspondence between local officials and the king occupy Ezra 4:7-22 and 5:6 - 6:12, and Ezra's letter of appointment from Artaxerxes is preserved in 7:12-26. The official language for such communications was Aramaic; which brings us to the next section.

### c. The languages employed

The two canonical books are in Hebrew, except for two sections, Ezra 4:8 - 6:18 and 7:12-26, which are in Aramaic. There is an obvious reason for most of this, for the material chiefly consists of copies of official correspondence, for which Aramaic was the standard language. Brockington points out that 52 out of the 67 verses come in this category, leaving only 15 as connecting passages. As to the reason for the retention of Aramaic for these narrative links, three suggestions have some degree of plausibility: *a.* that the Aramaic material is extracted from a history of the period, written in that language; *b.* that it consists of (in L. E. Browne's words) 'notes prepared for an advocate at some later time, . . . when the Jews were seeking some favour at court, to show that their loyalty had always been recognized';[1] *c.* that since the author and his readers were bilingual (otherwise the letters would have needed translation instead of simple inclusion), the short connecting passages were written in Aramaic to avoid too many transitions from one language to another. Although one may wonder why in that case the last four verses of Ezra 6 revert to Hebrew (chapter 7 marks a new section of the book), the third suggestion nevertheless seems the strongest since it requires no postulating of hypothetical documents.

### d. The authorship of the books

It has long been taken for granted that Chronicles, Ezra and Nehemiah are the work of one and the same author, called for convenience the Chronicler. Not only does Ezra begin where 2 Chronicles leaves off, even repeating the latter's final paragraph, but the style and outlook of these books seem at first sight virtually identical, except where the personal memoirs of Nehemiah strike their own distinctive note. The matter seemed clinched by S. R. Driver's formidable lists of words and constructions which are characteristic of this literature.[2]

A much closer look at the question, however, was taken in an article by Sara Japhet, 'The Supposed Common Authorship of Chronicles and Ezra–Nehemiah',[3] and more recently by H. G. M. Williamson in his book, *Israel in the Books of Chronicles* (CUP, 1977), leading to the conclusion that while these books share the general stylistic features of their post-exilic time, over against narrative works of other periods, they differ markedly among themselves (that is, Chronicles from Ezra–Nehemiah) in numerous matters of language and interests. Driver's word-list, supplemented by Curtis and Madsen in *ICC*, being designed to show the contrast between this literature and earlier books of the Old Testament, contained a large number of examples (Williamson finds 47) of words found in either one work or the

[1] *Peake's Commentary*, Revised (Nelson, 1962), p. 371.
[2] S. R. Driver, *Introduction to the Literature of the Old Testament* (T. & T. Clark, [7]1898), pp. 535–540.
[3] *VT* 18 (1968), pp. 330–371.

other in a special sense (*i.e.*, in Chronicles or in Ezra–Nehemiah), but not in both; which are therefore irrelevant to our particular question. Among the rest, many appear to 'favour diversity of authorship'[1] rather than unity. Under the microscope, so to speak, the contrast between Chronicles and Ezra–Nehemiah in habits of speech stands out with some clarity, showing divergent preferences concerning, for instance, the shorter or longer forms of certain classes of words,[2] or favourite adverbs, synonyms for cultic terms, and introductory formulae.

Not only these linguistic fingerprints but also broader considerations point to a separate author-compiler for Chronicles. Williamson points out, for instance, that the burning issue of mixed marriages in Ezra–Nehemiah is not an issue in Chronicles, which is even silent on Solomon's fatal example in this realm, to which Nehemiah drew attention (Ne. 13:26). Again, while 2 Kings 17:24ff. and Ezra 4:2, 10 tell of the foreigners disastrously imported into Israel by the kings of Assyria, Chronicles has not found room for the subject, though it was to cast so long a shadow over the returned exiles.

A further point is the odd arrangement of these books in the Hebrew Bible, whereby Chronicles *follows* Ezra and Nehemiah, to become the last book of the Old Testament. The only satisfactory explanation is that it was written later, for there is no evidence that (as some have suggested) it was initially excluded from the canon and only admitted later.[3] The fact that the final paragraph of Chronicles points the reader firmly to Ezra for the sequel can be argued either way; for while it makes a firm bond between the books it is also true that, as Welch remarked, 'men do not take the trouble to stitch together two documents unless they have been originally separate'.[4]

We conclude, then, that the compiler of Ezra–Nehemiah is unlikely to have been the Chronicler. Beyond that, one can note

[1] Williamson, p. 59.

[2] *E.g.*, among Japhet's many instances, the lengthened form of the 1st person imperf. consec. (ending in -*â*) occurs 50 times in Ezr.-Ne., but never in Ch. Again, while Ch. has various forms of theophoric names (ending in -*yāhû*, -*yô* or -*yāh*), in Ezr.-Ne. they are always written as -*yāh*. See further, Japhet, *passim*.

[3] The suggested reason for this hypothetical exclusion is that it duplicated other material. But as Williamson points out (pp. 10f.), such an objection was no bar to the inclusion of other and closer duplicates (*e.g.*, Is. 36f. with 2 Ki. 18:13ff.).

[4] A. C. Welch, *Post-Exilic Judaism* (Blackwood, 1935), p. 186, cited by Williamson, p. 7.

the Talmud's tradition, for what it is worth, that Ezra was the author (Baba Bathra 15a). This could well be so, if the argument of the next paragraphs about the probable date of the work is sound, for it has often been pointed out that Ezra's personal memoirs, unlike Nehemiah's, have very much the tone and style of the editorial material. But we need to remember that the last word on this subject must be the fact that the author has seen fit to leave his work anonymous.

As to the date of composition, opinions can only be tentative, and it is easier to arrive at the earliest date at which Ezra–Nehemiah could have been completed than to speak with any certainty beyond that.

Our estimate of this earliest date will of course be affected by our answer to the question whether Ezra lived in the reign of Artaxerxes I or that of Artaxerxes II, which is discussed on pp. 146ff., below. If we decide on the latter reign, it will imply a date fairly far down the 4th century, to allow time for memories to have faded enough for Ezra to have been considered a contemporary of Nehemiah. For so radical an error to have gone unnoticed we might well need to bring the date of writing still further down, say to the 3rd century. There is then, however, the question why the lists of names in Nehemiah stop short of such a time.

If on the other hand we decide that there was no confusion of chronology, either in Ezra 4 (see the opening comments on that chapter) or in the portrayal of Ezra and Nehemiah as contemporaries, we shall not need to postulate any appreciable interval between the events and their recording. On this view, which I support (see p. 158 and the discussion which it concludes), the books could have been compiled at any time from the last years of Darius II (423–404) onward.

A pivotal name for this matter is that of Jaddua in Nehemiah 12, since Josephus tells of a high priest of this name who saw the fall of the Persian empire to Alexander the Great in 331 BC. But I give reasons elsewhere for dissociating the Jaddua of that story from the Jaddua-ben-Jonathan of Nehemiah 12:11, 22, the successor but not the son of Johanan.[1] Freed from Josephus, Jaddua is seen to have flourished at about the turn of the 5th and 4th centuries BC, and the book of Ezra–Nehemiah could

[1] See pp. 144ff., and the commentary on Ne. 12:11. For a full discussion see H. G. M. Williamson, 'The Historical Value of Josephus' Jewish Antiquities XI. 297-301', in *JTS* (NS) 28 (1977), pp. 49-66. I am much indebted to this article.

accordingly have been written (or its lists brought up to date) at any time after his taking office.

Sheshbazzar is mentioned by name in only two paragraphs. In Ezra 1:8-11 Cyrus entrusts him with the vessels and with the task of rebuilding the Temple. In Ezra 5:14-16 a Jewish report recalls this and speaks of his appointment by Cyrus as governor (*peḥâ*), adding that he duly laid the Temple foundations. Nowhere else does the narrative mention him. Instead, it speaks of Zerubbabel as joint leader of the community with Jeshua the high priest. These are the names that meet us at the homecoming (Ezr. 2:2), at the foundation laying (3:8), at the confrontation (4:2ff.) and eventually at the resumption of the project (5:2). And at this point Zerubbabel is referred to as governor (*peḥâ*) in Haggai 1:1, which is the title previously borne by Sheshbazzar (Ezr. 5:14).

Several theories have been offered to account for this.

**1.** A view of long standing is that Sheshbazzar was but another name, perhaps a court name, for Zerubbabel, as Belteshazzar was for Daniel. Against this is the lack of any explanatory note to this effect, and especially the manner in which Zerubbabel and his fellow elders refer to Sheshbazzar as apparently a figure of the past in their statement to the authorities ('. . . one whose name was Sheshbazzar', 5:14; '. . .Then this Sheshbazzar came', 5:16), when it would have strengthened their hand to identify him as being still their leader. Another point against it is that both these names appear to be Babylonian,[1] whereas Daniel's name was given him to replace an Israelite one. Yet this is not a fatal objection, since the name Zedekiah is an example of an official appellation which was drawn from the same culture as the name which it replaced (2 Ki. 24:17). Even the lack of any note to identify the two would not be without precedent: *cf.* the names Azariah and Uzziah, which are nowhere brought together yet are used in 2 Kings 15 interchangeably, the former seven times and the latter four times. In Ezra the variations could be dictated by the contexts: Sheshbazzar in imperial settings, Zerubbabel in Jewish ones. A variant of this theory is that the two names are two abbreviations

---

[1] But Brockington (p. 53) argues that Zerubbabel could as easily be a Heb. name (shortened from *zᵉrūᵃ bāḇel*, 'born in Babylon') as a Babylonian one.

of a longer one: see the conjectural reconstruction by R. D. Wilson mentioned in *NBD* (art. Sheshbazzar).

**2.** Some of those who suspect the biblical author of improving on his sources have suggested that Zerubbabel and the main body of the exiles had been in no hurry to return and rebuild when Cyrus made his decree in 538, and only took up the challenge in the reign of Darius I (522–486), as recorded in Ezra 5 and 6 and in Haggai and Zechariah. To cover up this slow response (one form of the argument runs) our author made them return with the first trickle of homecomers, either identifying Zerubbabel with Sheshbazzar or leaving their relationship an open question, and blamed the delay over the rebuilding not on their failure to start but upon their being forced to stop.

One good witness and one dubious one are appealed to in support of this. Haggai, whose preaching in the year 520 spurred Zerubbabel and the rest into rebuilding the Temple, is a first-hand witness, and seems unaware of any previous work on the project. But this impression is partly due to translations which make him speak of laying the Temple's foundation (Hg. 2 : 18), which sounds like an absolute beginning; whereas in fact he used a more general term than this (*yāsaḏ*, to establish or repair[1]). It also overlooks the moral realities of the situation presented in Ezra, which demanded of Haggai a preacher's emphasis on the shame of the present rather than on the traces of the past. Those traces, in any case, would have been minimal after nearly two decades of neglect. To rebuild now was in effect a pioneer work, whatever had been briefly started in the days of Cyrus.

The other witness is the apocryphal 1 Esdras, which inserts between (approximately) Ezra 1 and 2[2] the entertaining story of a speech-making contest between three guardsmen of King Darius. One of the speakers, the winner, is Zerubbabel, who chooses for his prize the privilege of reminding Darius of his vow and Cyrus's, to return the sacred vessels to Jerusalem and to have the Temple rebuilt. Although the vessels have already been safely returned by Cyrus to Sheshbazzar in an earlier chapter of

---

[1] While it can certainly mean to lay foundations, it is also used of Joash's repair work in 2 Ch. 24:27. For a discussion of this verb, see A. Gelston, 'The Foundations of the Second Temple', *VT* 16 (1966), pp. 232–235; also F. I. Andersen, 'Who built the second Temple?', *Australian Biblical Review* 6 (1958), esp. pp. 13–27.

[2] More exactly, between Ezr. 1 plus 4 : 7–24, and Ezr. 2.

the same book (1 Esdras 2 : 14), the narrator seems unaware that he has said so, and now has them returned by Darius (1 Esdras 4 : 57), who sends Zerubbabel with a great company of returning exiles to Jerusalem. The story then comes back mainly into step with Ezra 2ff., and indeed back to the reign of Cyrus. It may be consciously retrospective here (though it does not give that impression); but even if this is so, it still manages to make Darius become king only two years after the death of Cyrus (1 Esdras 5 : 73).

The only evidential value seriously claimed for this story is that it may point, however confusedly, to the existence of a variant tradition about the date of Zerubbabel's return. This is of course conceivable, but it treats this mixture of fantasy and self-contradiction more seriously than it deserves. It is simpler, and accounts for more of the data, to conclude that the author or reviser of 1 Esdras could not resist a good story, and inserted it at a carelessly chosen point into a narrative with which it had nothing to do.

**3.** A third view is that Sheshbazzar and Zerubbabel were respectively the official and unofficial leaders of the first wave of settlers. In the eyes of government, and in any report submitted to it, Sheshbazzar would be responsible for everything that was done; yet for a positive lead the people would have looked to Zerubbabel and Jeshua, their own men and descendants of their kings and priests. So in Ezra 3 the rebuilding attempt is rightly credited to them, whereas in 5 : 14–16, with equal justification, it is reported to the authorities as the work of Sheshbazzar, whose official responsibility it was, and whose name rather than theirs could be verified from the archives (5 : 17). Later, and certainly by 520 BC, Zerubbabel himself was appointed governor (Hg. 1 : 1).

One question raised by this interpretation is Sheshbazzar's nationality. If he was a Babylonian it was natural for the real leadership to come chiefly from elsewhere: from the princely Zerubbabel and priestly Jeshua. But he is called 'the prince of Judah' (1 : 8), and while this Hebrew term (*nāśî'*) is not a royal title it does suggest that he stood high in the Jewish community. It is the term used of the old tribal leaders (Nu. 1 : 16) and is taken up by Ezekiel for the Davidic messiah (Ezk. 34 : 24). Although this is not conclusive, since *ha-nāśî' lîhûdâ* could perhaps be translated 'the one set up for Judah' (thus a Hebrew alternative for the foreign terms used elsewhere for 'governor'), this is somewhat forced. The normal meaning is a native prince or chief, not an alien official.[1]

If this man was a Jew, however, as he seems to have been, why was he given precedence over Zerubbabel, who was of royal descent? The answer may be that the Persians hesitated to appoint a potential claimant to the throne, preferring at this stage a man who would command respect but not enthusiasm. A quite different suggestion, which has enjoyed fairly wide support, is that Sheshbazzar was himself of royal blood, being none other than Shenazzar, an uncle of Zerubbabel (1 Ch. 3:18). The almost endless variations on the name Sheshbazzar in the Greek versions lend some plausibility to this,[2] but it has recently been shown beyond reasonable doubt that in the Hebrew text (as C. C. Torrey had claimed as long ago as 1920) the two names in question, Sheshbazzar and Shenazzar, are 'correctly transmitted and perfectly distinct'. The conjecture is thus left without the evidence—meagre at best—to which it had appealed.[3]

A final and perhaps decisive fact is that Sheshbazzar is given no family identity. This is a further objection, if one were needed, to identifying him with Shenazzar son of King Jehoiachin; but it also counts against his being a Jew of high standing. We are therefore left, it seems, with only two viable alternatives: either that he was a foreign official (if the title 'prince of Judah' can legitimately mean 'governor'), or that in spite of the silences of the narrative, Sheshbazzar was the official name of Zerubbabel, whose pedigree is only given when he is mentioned under his own name.

Between these alternatives I find it hard to judge, but am marginally drawn to the former.

[1] Ezk. (*e.g.*, 12:10, 12) uses it regularly of Zedekiah, the puppet of Nebuchadrezzar who held the true king captive. But Zedekiah was Jewish, and royal. For the *nāśī'* in Ezk. 40–48 see H. Gese, '*Der Verfassungsentwurf des Ezechiel'*, *Beiträge zur historischen Theologie*, 25 (1957), esp. pp. 116f. For the view that it was used of Abraham as holding authority from God, his sovereign, see D. J. Wiseman, 'Abraham the Prince', *Bibliotheca Sacra* 134 (1977), esp. p. 233.

[2] The nearest approach to the Greek 'Sanesar' of 1 Ch. 3:18, LXX, is 'Sanamassar' or 'Sanabassar' in 1 Esdras (Esdras A) 2:11.

[3] See P. R. Berger, *ZAW* 83 (1971), pp. 98–100, who points out that there is now direct inscriptional evidence of the variant form *šaššu* for *šamaš* (the Babylonian sun god) and thereby of the validity of the Hebraized name Sheshbazzar (for *šaššu-aba-uṣur*, 'may *šamaš/šaššu* protect the father') which therefore needs no explanation in terms of the moon god *sîn* or of the name Shenazzar. Torrey's dictum, quoted by Berger, is in *AJSL* 37 (1920/21), p. 93 n. 1.

III. THE ELEPHANTINE PAPYRI AND SOME STATEMENTS OF JOSEPHUS

Occasional references are made in the commentary to the Elephantine papyri, a collection of Aramaic documents (largely legal and business letters) found at Aswan at the southern border of Egypt. The name Elephantine refers to a small island in the Nile at that point, also named Yeb, on which a military colony of Jews was settled—perhaps originally mercenaries but, by the time of these documents of the 5th century BC, an established community with wives and families and property.

A reference to the sparing of their temple when Cambyses had destroyed many Egyptian temples (525 BC) suggests that the community was already of quite long standing at the beginning of the Persian period, and we are reminded that Egypt had seemed a natural haven to the Jews of Jeremiah's time, early in the 6th century. Like Jeremiah's abductors (Je. 43:5-7; 44:15ff.) these expatriates were far from orthodox, blithely coupling the name of Yahweh with gods and goddesses of Canaan. As such, they provide a clear sample of unreformed Judaism, to set alongside that of the reformed community which came back chastened from Babylon, to be further educated under Ezra and Nehemiah. Like the local deputation which approached Zerubbabel in Ezra 4:1ff., they would have protested, 'We worship your God as you do'; but their documents help us to see how serious a theological difference that phrase could conceal. As A. Cowley has pointed out, Judaism as we know it 'is the natural growth of the system born under Ezra: it could not have grown out of a religious system such as that of the colonists of Elephantine'.[1] It may be significant that this group appealed for help to both Jerusalem and Samaria on one occasion, and was certainly rebuffed by the former. In a letter of 407[2] BC to Bagohi, governor of Judah, requesting his support for their efforts to get their temple rebuilt after a pogrom, the colonists complain that Johanan the high priest and his colleagues in Jerusalem have ignored their appeal of three years earlier, and that they have written also 'to Delaiah and Shelemiah the sons of Sanballat governor of Samaria'.

This same letter happens to be important also for the history of the times. *a.* It reveals the status of Sanballat, and by implying that by 407 BC he was governor in little more than name, with his

---

[1] A. Cowley, *Aramaic Papyri of the Fifth Century B.C.* (Oxford, 1923), p. xxviii.
[2] Cowley, No. 30, pp. 108-119.

sons acting for him, it dovetails with Nehemiah's account of him in his prime in 445, thereby helping to confirm that Nehemiah's patron was Artaxerxes I (464–423) rather than Artaxerxes II (404–359). b. On the other hand, the mention of Johanan as high priest in 410 is an important datum for those who argue that Ezra followed rather than preceded Nehemiah (see pp. 153ff.). c. The name Bagohi, governor of Judah, introduces us to a series of identifications of people and events by Josephus (*Ant.* xi. 7, 8), who uses a Greek form of the name, *viz.*, Bagoses. Josephus makes the high priest, Joannes (*i.e.*, Johanan), the son rather than brother of Joiada, son of Eliashib,[1] and records that he had a brother named Jesus for whom Bagoses planned to obtain the high priesthood. In the course of a quarrel Joannes killed Jesus in the temple, whereupon Bagoses imposed a seven-year punishment on the Jewish people. Josephus, who has identified Bagoses as 'the general of another Artaxerxes', goes on to tell of the high priesthood of Jaddua, son of Joannes, who also came into conflict with his own brother. This brother, Manasses, married Nikaso the daughter of Sanballat who 'had been sent to Samaria as satrap by Darius the last king'. The marriage scandalized the Jewish elders, who gave Manasses the choice between divorcing his wife and forfeiting the priesthood. But Sanballat had the last word by building a temple on mount Gerizim for his son-in-law, with the consent of Alexander the Great to whom he had now transferred his allegiance.

This takes us far beyond the Elephantine papyri or the book of Nehemiah, but it has enough names in common with both of these to create a tangle which calls for some unravelling.

The first thing that needs to be said is that the Elephantine letter is first-hand evidence that three people whose names recur in the Josephus passage, *viz.*, Johanan (Greek: Joannes), Bagohi (Bagoses) and Sanballat (Sanaballates), were in office when we encounter them in the fourteenth and seventeenth years of Darius II (*i.e.*, 410 and 407 BC).

Secondly, Nehemiah tells of a member of the high-priestly family, a son of Jehoiada-ben-Eliashib, who became son-in-law to Sanballat and was 'chased' from Nehemiah's presence, not long after 432 BC (Ne. 13 : 6f., 28).

Thirdly, Josephus firmly dates his story of a schismatic son-in-law of Sanballat at the point when Alexander was taking over

---

[1] This assumption is criticized on p. 154.

the Persian empire, *i.e.*, *c.* 331 BC, a century after Nehemiah's incident.

So we are left with two possibilities with regard to this part of Josephus's account: either history has largely repeated itself, or Josephus has scrambled his chronology. Indeed there could be elements of both, for the fact that in several prominent families of this period, including that of Sanballat, certain names keep recurring in alternate generations (see the remarks and footnote on the Samaria papyri, above, p. 16), produces confusing similarities between certain events, and Josephus betrays elsewhere some misunderstandings of the Persian period.[1] What is out of the question is that the Sanballat of Josephus has any chronological light to throw on the Sanballat of Nehemiah and the Elephantine papyri.

That being so, it would be rash to rely on Josephus's other identifications, whereby the Jaddua whom he names as high priest at the fall of the Persian empire in 331 was the son and immediate successor of the Joannes/Johanan whom we know to have been in office in 410, nearly eighty years before. Both the chronology and the tendency of family names to recur at intervals make it more likely that the Joannes and Jaddua of Josephus lived under the last kings of Persia and are distinct from those of Nehemiah 12:11, 22. In any case, the biblical Jaddua was the son of Jonathan, not of Johanan (see the commentary).

The fact that Bagoses/Bagohi and Johanan are names linked together in both Josephus and the papyri may seem to conflict with this; but both were common names,[2] and the former is qualified in the papyri by the information that its bearer was governor (*peḥâ*) of Judah under Darius (II), whereas in Josephus he is 'the general (*stratēgos*) of the other Artaxerxes' (though he is clearly implied to have civil power as well). He could be the same man in both contexts, if 'the other Artaxerxes' means Artaxerxes II (404-359), who followed Darius; but the chronological improbability mentioned above concerning Joannes and Jaddua makes it somewhat easier, in my view, to connect this Bagoses with Artaxerxes III (359/8-338/7), which brings him nearer to the next events in Josephus. If so, it is conceivable that he was the Persian general Bagoas, an aggressive and ambitious character

---

[1] See H. G. M. Williamson, *JTS* (NS) 28 (1977), pp. 49-66.

[2] A variant spelling of the former is Bigvai, Ezr. 2:2=Ne. 7:7; Ezr. 2:14=Ne. 7:19; Ezr. 8:14; Ne. 10:16. It is a Persian name, compounded with 'Baga', 'God', and borne by Jews as well as Persians.

who rose to great power and influence with Artaxerxes III, and at one time 'administered all the king's affairs in the upper satrapies' according to Diodorus Siculus[1] (who does not, however, identify these regions more closely). But so common a name and such scanty data leave the question wide open.

For a fuller discussion of the Josephus statements see the article by H. G. M. Williamson, referred to above. Meanwhile enough may have been said to show that while Josephus brings us knowledge of events and personalities of which we would otherwise have been ignorant, his chronological scheme for them is too questionable to be made a basis for rearranging the canonical history.

## IV. A QUESTION OF CHRONOLOGY: EZRA-NEHEMIAH OR NEHEMIAH-EZRA?

A suggestion made in passing by M. Vernes in 1889, followed by a monograph by A. van Hoonacker in 1890, raised the question whether Ezra and Nehemiah both served the same King Artaxerxes or should rather be assigned to different reigns— Nehemiah to Artaxerxes I (464–423) and Ezra to Artaxerxes II (404–359). It was a seed-thought which was to grow and proliferate with extraordinary vigour. Within twenty years there had sprung up several new propositions: that Ezra's mission had started not in the seventh year of either of these kings but in the thirty-second year of Artaxerxes I (Kosters, 1895), or the twenty-seventh (Cheyne, 1902), or, still within that reign, at some time between the two visits of Nehemiah (Kennett, 1909); while C. C. Torrey had followed up a still more radical hypothesis of Vernes, that Ezra was a figment of the Chronicler's imagination. Other suggestions were to come, dating Ezra, for example, in the thirty-seventh year of Artaxerxes I (*e.g.*, Albright, 1946; A. Pavlovský, 1957), or exchanging Ezra's date with Nehemiah's, so that Nehemiah came to Jerusalem in the seventh year and Ezra in the twentieth (Jellicoe, 1947). But van Hoonacker's thesis, retaining the regnal years of the text while attaching them to two different kings, has continued to have many supporters.[2]

[1] Diodorus Siculus, XVI. 47, 49, 50. *Cf.* XVII. 5.
[2] See, *e.g.*, J. A. Emerton, 'Did Ezra go to Jerusalem in 428 BC?', *JTS* (NS) 17 (1956), pp. 1–19. For convenient surveys of the debate, see H. H. Rowley, *The Servant of the Lord* (Lutterworth, 1952), pp. 131–159, and *Men of God*, pp. 211–245. More recently, U. Kellermann in *ZAW* 80 (1968), pp. 55–87 (a very thorough guide); R. W. Klein in F. M. Cross *et al.*, *Magnalia Dei* (Doubleday, 1976),

With a few exceptions, there is general agreement that Nehemiah's dates, as against those of Ezra, are secure (*viz.*, 445-433 for his first period as governor, and some time shortly after this for his second), since the Elephantine papyri offer incidental support for their general accuracy.[1] It is also agreed that the chronological reconstructions which would make Nehemiah arrive before Ezra involve some rewriting of the biblical narrative, not simply a reinterpretation of it. The text as it stands precludes such a sequence, and is therefore emended at certain points in the belief that the author or final editor has, in H. H. Rowley's phrase, 'slightly touched up the story'.[2] Whether it is in fact the ancient writer or the modern scholar who deserves this comment is what we must now consider.

The thread that runs through all this diversity of hypotheses is the unacceptability, in the judgment of those who take these views, of the temporal priority of Ezra over Nehemiah, although some would allow him to have arrived towards the end of Nehemiah's career, and therefore to have had some dealings with him. And while many grounds are given for these rearrangements of events, most of their advocates give precedence to the same four apparent anomalies in the story, namely: *a.* the comparative lack of combined activity by the two reformers; *b.* the thirteen-year gap between Ezra's arrival and his reported reading of the law; *c.* Nehemiah's seeming unawareness of Ezra's divorce machinery; *d.* a series of contacts with the high priest Eliashib and his successors, which seem to place Nehemiah and Ezra a generation or two apart. There are also minor points, generally agreed to be inconclusive, and worth discussing only after these first four, to which we now turn.

---

pp. 370ff. (see also his survey, pp. 361ff., of other aspects of the current study of Ezra–Nehemiah). For a well-argued defence of the biblical chronology see J. S. Wright, *The Date of Ezra's Coming to Jerusalem* (Tyndale Press, [2]1958; reissued by the Theological Students' Fellowship, 1978); also, although based only on Ezr. 7:12-26, U. Kellermann, as above.

[1] For some details of these papyri, see pp. 143ff. They have a bearing on Nehemiah's dates in that they imply that Sanballat, who had been Nehemiah's vigorous opponent in the reign of Artaxerxes, was an old man when a certain letter was written in 407 BC. They also show that in 410 the Jerusalem high priest was Johanan, who is implied in Ne. 12:22 to have been the second successor to Nehemiah's contemporary, Eliashib.

[2] H. H. Rowley, *Men of God*, p. 233.

*a. Infrequent co-operation*

It is often felt to be surprising that these two outstanding men, dedicated to the same ends and armed with royal authority in their respective spheres, should be seen so seldom together in concerted action. True, we read that after Nehemiah's rebuilding of the defences Ezra was called upon to read the law (Ne. 8: 1ff.); that Nehemiah helped to guide the people's response to it (8:9), and headed the list of those who sealed the ensuing covenant (10 : 1); also that at the dedication of the wall the two men took prominent parts in the twin processions (12:31, 36, 38, 40). This, on the face of it, is ample evidence that Ezra and Nehemiah overlapped in time and place, and that each publicly supported the distinctive achievement of the other—Nehemiah the proclamation of the law, and Ezra the completion of the wall. To have expected a more active partnership than this is understandable enough, but to demand it as a condition of believing that they were contemporaries is unreasonable; all the more so when the unknown factors in a situation so largely inaccessible to us are literally innumerable.

It is possible, though, to challenge this evidence for their joint appearances.

1. *Textually*, the external witness is not unanimous, for there are variants in the Greek translation (LXX) of the above references. Two of these variants are minimal: in Nehemiah 8:9 and 10:1 (2, MT) LXX omits '(who was) the governor' (lit. 'the Tirshatha', RV) after Nehemiah's name (though 1 Esdras 9:49, by doing the opposite, indicates that 'the Tirshatha' was indeed in the Hebrew text of Ne. 8:9). In Nehemiah 12, however, LXX not only has a shorter text (omitting verse 38 and a fragment on either side of it, also verses 39c–42c) but has 'they' instead of Nehemiah's 'I' in verse 31—so that in this translation of the Old Testament Nehemiah disappears from the record of the dedication.[1] On the other hand, even in the uncorrected text of LXX Ezra is present (Ne. 12:36); and his is the crucial name, for it is his presence rather than Nehemiah's which could not have been taken for granted on this great day. It would therefore be somewhat desperate pleading to dismiss the record of partnership on these grounds.

2. *Grammatically*, an objection has been raised to Nehemiah 8:9, in that the verb 'said' is singular, and its subject plural,

---

[1] In the margin of Codex Sinaiticus, however, the missing verses are written in.

which Brockington considers 'a violation of grammatical usage' (p. 30) and therefore a sign that Nehemiah and the Levites were not originally mentioned in this verse. But this construction is not only possible but quite normal when the verb (as here) *precedes* a string of subjects. Gesenius, noting that this use of the third masculine singular occurs 'very frequently' (G-K 145 *o*), cites four examples in the middle chapters of Genesis alone (Gn. 12 : 16, *etc.*) of its employment 'before collectives and mixed subjects'. An occurrence which is conveniently near at hand for reference is in Ezra 8 : 20, where 'David and his officials' share a verb in the third singular as here. The objection therefore has no force, unless a further appeal is made to verse 10 on the assumption (which begs the question) that Ezra was originally the subject of that verse.[1]

The passages which couple the two names are in fact queried chiefly on broader grounds. The objection is partly that (as we have seen) to some minds they depict an unacceptably small degree of co-operation between Ezra and Nehemiah, and partly that these references are an inconvenient obstacle to any wholesale rearrangement of the story. The fact that these fragments of data are quite few, and could be cut away from the text with only minor surgery, makes them all the more provocative. So, *e.g.*, H. H. Rowley:

> 'These passages' [*viz.*, where the names of Ezra and Nehemiah stand together] 'are quite insufficient to convince us that Ezra and Nehemiah were dominant figures living and working side by side in Jerusalem, each acting independently on the same questions. Wherever their names are found together one is a mere passenger, whose name can be dropped without the slightest consequence to the narrative.'[2]

This, however, is both subjective ('insufficient to convince us') and arbitrary ('. . . can be dropped without the slightest

---

[1] J. A. Emerton in *JTS* (NS) 17 (1966), p. 15, accordingly finds no grammatical difficulty in verse 9, though he regards the singular verb in verse 10 as pointing to Ezra as the probable subject of both verses. This, however, is not the requirement of the text itself, which makes Nehemiah the one who intervened, supported by his colleagues, and who by implication gave the constructive injunctions of verse 10. If, for the sake of argument, any names had to be removed from verse 9 as secondary, the word-order would point to excising Ezra and the Levites, rather than Nehemiah.

[2] *The Servant of the Lord*, p. 156.

consequence to the narrative'), and one cannot rewrite one's sources on such principles. To be fair, those who suggest that we should do this would not resort to it without additional reasons, for they see Ezra's relationship with Nehemiah as only one of several interlocking problems.

## b. The thirteen-year gap

This is the implied interval between Ezra's arrival in Jerusalem in the seventh year of Artaxerxes to administer the law (Ezr. 7:8), and his public reading of it in the twentieth year, as recorded in Nehemiah 8 (cf. Ne. 2:1).

If we persuade ourselves that this public occasion was Ezra's first move towards carrying out his task, we shall find a huge anomaly here. We shall return to this crucial 'if' in the final paragraph of this section. But first, how sure can we be of these thirteen years?

Certainly the compiler of Ezra–Nehemiah vouches for them. Against this, it has been suggested that, whether by inadvertence or by a desire to follow a theme rather than a time-sequence, he has put chapters 8–10 of Nehemiah at a place which they did not originally occupy in his source. But this is not tenable unless the text is emended, since Nehemiah's own presence anchors these chapters (Ne. 8–10) to the reign of Artaxerxes I[1] and to at least the twentieth year of it, 445 BC. If, however, his name were cut out from these chapters (and Ezra's from Ne. 12:36) on the grounds discussed in section 1, the chapters themselves (Ne. 8–10) could be moved bodily back to the book of Ezra, to follow either Ezra 8 (in the 4½ months between Ezra's arrival and the events of chapter 9) or Ezra 10, where they would give a more positive ending to the book. This would allow Ezra's mission to be dated without reference to that of Nehemiah, and the reading of the law to be placed at any time after his arrival that seemed convenient. Nor would this rearrangement be without visible support. The apocryphal book 1 Esdras continues the story of Ezra in the second of these ways, moving straight on from the equivalent of Ezra 10 (the divorce proceedings) to that of Nehemiah 8:1–12 or 13a (the reading of the law), where it breaks off. This, too, is the order followed by Josephus, who finishes his account of Ezra with this event (and a note of Ezra's old age and death), before turning to the history of Nehemiah.

---

[1] Reasons for dating Nehemiah in this reign are given on p. 147.

The question that matters, however, is *why* these authors adopt this order. Did they have independent access to the history, or did the author of 1 Esdras (which Josephus follows)[1] judge it best to round off the story of one reformer before (or without) introducing that of the other? The second of these alternatives is quite sufficient to account for what we find, especially if in fact his book, which breaks off at this point, was never intended to take us beyond the career of Ezra. And while this additional possibility cannot be proved, the claim that 1 Esdras may go back to a source whose order of events differed from that of Scripture has now been effectively refuted. H. G. M. Williamson has shown that the context of 1 Esdras 9 : 37 makes it clear that the author was using a document in which, as in the Bible, Nehemiah 8 followed Nehemiah 7, not Ezra 10.[2]

The way is therefore open for a fresh look at the biblical evidence itself. Upon this, the fact emerges, perhaps surprisingly in view of the arguments and counter-arguments, that on this point at least (the thirteen-year gap between Ezra 8 and Nehemiah 8) there is no problem at all in the text—only in what is commonly read into it. The thirteen years are there, but there is no suggestion that they were silent years: this only arises from the assumption that Ezra produced the law book for the first time at this great rally. The assumption is doubly gratuitous in that it would limit him to a particular medium of instruction and, within that medium, to this particular occasion for his first use of it.[3]

This trespass on the silence of the text is a tacit denial of the historian's right, indeed necessity, to choose what he will record or discard. Yet it would be hard to fault this narrator on his

---

[1] One reason for Josephus's preference may be that 1 Esdras includes the entertaining story of the three guardsmen in his parallel to Ezr. 1–6. A further reason may have been the more manageable narrative which 1 Esdras offered by going on to the climax of Ezra's work before embarking (if indeed it ever did) on Nehemiah's.

[2] H. G. M. Williamson, *Israel in the Books of Chronicles* (CUP, 1977), p. 36.

[3] The wide currency of this assumption is probably a legacy of early pentateuchal criticism, which held that what Ezra brought to Jerusalem was the newly- (or nearly-) completed Pentateuch. In that case, his first step would doubtless have been to call a public assembly and win acceptance for the new law; and this is what Ne. 8 is said to record in the wrong context. Among recent commentators there is more reserve over this view of Ezra as an innovator (*cf.*, *e.g.*, Brockington, p. 23); nevertheless its influence persists, not least in perpetuating the assumptions we have noted above. See Appendix V, pp. 158–164.

choice of significant episodes for Ezra: the crisis over foreign wives in his first year of office, and the Torah celebration to round off his career. The objection also makes too little of the witness of Ezra 9:1ff., where it is clear that on his arrival Ezra had pressed vigorously ahead with his mission. The concern of the officials who reported the mixed marriages; the influence of the Pentateuch on their language in doing so (see the commentary on Ezr. 9:1, 2); the sensitivity of the people to Ezra's consequent distress, and their extraordinary readiness to make amends, all clearly imply a recent and powerful campaign of education in the law. Ezra's supposed inaction for thirteen years is the last thing that could properly be read out of this account. If one chooses to read *into* it the events of Nehemiah 8–10, amended and transposed, it can of course be done on those terms; but it is not the text which requires that exercise.

*c. Nehemiah's handling of mixed marriages*

Ezra's approach (Ezr. 10:10ff.) to this problem was radical: the evil must be cut out by divorce. Why then was Nehemiah content with so much less: simply a rough encounter and the extraction of an oath against repeating the offence (Ne. 13:23ff.)? With Ezra's precedent behind him he could have set up court and had these marriages and many more dissolved. Could the answer be that the sequence of events is wrong, and that Nehemiah was the first to meet the trouble? In that case an improvised and local approach was tried, found wanting and replaced by Ezra's legal action—a plausible progression.

A further argument, which weighs heavily with some writers, is that the biblical account (in their view) hardly tallies with the immense reputation of Ezra. In the words of John Bright:

' ... any theory placing Ezra's reforms (Ezra, chs. 9:10) before Nehemiah's inevitably involves the conclusion that Ezra in one way or another failed. ... That Ezra was a failure is, to me, unbelievable. Not only does the Bible not so paint him, the whole course of Judaism was shaped by his work. Would this have been the case, and would tradition have made of him no less than a second Moses, had he been a failure? Yet so he was if his reforms preceded those of Nehemiah.'[1]

[1] J. Bright, *A History of Israel* (SCM, ²1972), p. 394.

I find both these arguments surprising. As to the first, there is a certain neatness in the idea of an upward progress from Nehemiah's rough and ready handling of a matter at the local level and face-to-face, to Ezra's settling of it nationwide and through the courts. But this is too simple. If we are to compare Ezra's reforms with Nehemiah's it is not enough to count heads or look at legal precedents. We are faced first with two contrasted personalities and styles of action, and then with a human situation far more complex than a few points of case-law. Ezra's major surgery was indeed highly efficient; but what of the flood of divorcees and uprooted children which it let loose on society? Any subsequent reformer would have had to choose between a repetition of this and the alternative of attempting less in the hope of achieving more. Which of these courses would constitute the lesser evil would have been far from self-evident.

The second argument—that if Ezra preceded Nehemiah he must be written off as a failure—is equally unrealistic, for it reckons without the cross-currents which any reformation will set in motion, and without the eroding effects of time. Every reform breeds its malcontents, tends to lose impetus, and is soon confronted with a new generation to convert. Those who argue that Ezra was no 'second Moses' if his people relapsed into old ways must have forgotten the story of the original Moses. It would in fact be hard to name any reformer or saviour whose work was not in this sense a failure; yet nobody will normally blame the reformer for the fickleness of his flock.

### d. Synchronisms with the high priest's family

This argument for the reversing of the traditional order of events is in outline very simple, if its facts are correct. It asserts that whereas Eliashib was high priest when Nehemiah came to Jerusalem (Ne. 3:1), Eliashib's grandson J(eh)ohanan was high priest when Ezra came. This, if so, makes Ezra later than Nehemiah by perhaps two generations, instead of earlier by thirteen years. Further, we know from the Elephantine papyri[1] that the high priest in 410 BC was named Johanan.

However, the evidence for the central pillars of this argument is weak. These pillars are the double assumption that Ezra's high priest was Johanan, and that Johanan was Eliashib's grandson.

To answer the second and less important of these suppositions

[1] See above, pp. 143ff.

first, the fact is that Johanan is named as Eliashib's son, not his grandson, in the two biblical statements of their relationship (Ezr. 10:6; Ne. 12:23).[1] True, 'son' can be used generically, of any descendant, but that is not its primary meaning, and those who understand it here as 'grandson' have to assume also that in Nehemiah 12:11 'Jonathan' ('Yahweh has given') is a scribal mistake for 'Johanan' ('Yahweh has shown mercy'). These two names are quite distinct from one another, whereas Jehohanan, Johanan and the Greek Joannes are all variants of one appellation, the source of our name John.[2] This part of the argument rests, then, on a secondary meaning ('grandson') and on an unsupported textual emendation, since LXX and the other ancient versions support the Hebrew text of Nehemiah 12:11 with the name Jonathan, not Johanan.

The other and major assumption is that Johanan was already high priest in Ezra's first year at Jerusalem. Its basis is the fact that Ezra, after his day of public lamentation outside the Temple, spent the night in 'the chamber of Jehohanan the son of Eliashib' (Ezr. 10:6). On this, Rowley makes the comment:

> 'In the context of events narrated in this chapter Ezra would not be expected to be consorting with subordinate officials and youths, but with the high priest, and ... it is most likely that it was as high priest that Johanan received him into his room.'[3]

If Johanan is regarded as Eliashib's grandson (see above) rather than his son, he would indeed have been 'a mere boy', as Ryle puts it,[4] in 458 BC; but this is an insecure assumption, as we have seen. If we are to keep strictly to the evidence, it is that Ezra used the room of *Jehohanan the son of Eliashib*—not naming Jehohanan

[1] On the liberties taken with these texts in certain modern versions, see the footnote to Ne. 12:22.

[2] Taking the biblical data to be correct, we see Eliashib with two sons, Joiada (Ne. 12:10) and Johanan (Ezr. 10:6; Ne. 12:23). Joiada was evidently succeeded not by his son Jonathan but by his brother Johanan (Ne. 12:22), and Johanan by Joiada's grandson Jaddua (Ne. 12:11, 22). We are not told what prevented Jonathan from succeeding his father Joiada—unless possibly Ne. 13:28 points to the answer, *i.e.*, that Jonathan was the renegade expelled by Nehemiah. But that is no more than one possibility out of any number of unknowns. On Josephus's statements about some of these names, see pp. 999.

[3] *The Servant of the Lord*, p. 146.

[4] But Ryle draws a different conclusion from Rowley's, namely that the writer is identifying the room for his readers by reference to its occupant in their day. *Cf.*, likewise, F. Ahlemann, *ZAW* 59 (1942/3), p. 98.

as high priest, nor as Eliashib's son's son, as we are asked to imagine. Moreover, the idea that Ezra would have scorned to consort with anyone less than the high priest has obviously not occurred to the biblical author; only to subsequent scholars, whose insight into Ezra's scale of values and into all the attendant circumstances may be less than perfect.

In recent works, indeed, even those who favour a late date for Ezra tend to treat this episode as an inconclusive part of their case. The summing-up by Coggins is judicious: 'In short, we may conclude that this verse fits in well with the theory that puts Ezra some fifty years after Nehemiah but is far from establishing it.'[1] This open verdict, or its like, is not confined to this part of the argument, or to one author. It can be paralleled from the summaries of the whole Ezra–Nehemiah question by a variety of writers who, while strongly committed to the revised chronology, regard it as more than probable but less than proven.[2]

From the four mainstays of the argument for Nehemiah's priority, we can now turn to some supplementary points which might have a bearing on the question, but which, as most agree, can bear little weight and can be argued—at best—either way.

1. John Bright (*A History of Israel*, p. 394) considers 'the disturbed early years of Artaxerxes I' a scarcely credible time for Ezra's unescorted but successful journey from Babylonia to Jerusalem. By merely human reckoning this may be true; yet even at this level it is not the whole truth, since unrest on the borders of the empire could well have spurred Artaxerxes to strengthen the agencies of law and order wherever he could; hence his despatch of Ezra to Judah. For Ezra's part, the refusal of an escort was an act of faith, as he tells us, and it should be judged as such. It is curious to find so earnest a defender of Ezra's spiritual stature as John Bright (see above, section 3) setting this limit to what he would have dared to do to prove his point to the king (Ezr. 8:21–23).

2. Ezra was thronged by crowds in Jerusalem in the year of his arrival, but Nehemiah found the city short of houses and inhabitants (Ne. 7:4), and took steps to repopulate it. So if Ezra

---

[1] Coggins, pp. 63f.
[2] See, e.g., M. Noth, *The History of Israel* (Black, [2]1960), p. 320; H. H. Rowley, *Men of God*, p. 232; J. Bright, *A History of Israel*, p. 380; and most modern commentaries. Recently, however, the traditional chronology has found renewed favour: see the articles by Kellermann and Klein noted on 'p. 146, n. 2.

were dated after Nehemiah we should have a steady progression from an empty city to a full one. This is attractive, but inconclusive, since in the first place Ezra's 'very great assembly' (Ezr. 10:1) is not said to have consisted of the local inhabitants. It had 'gathered to him out of Israel'—which points rather to the crowds who had come to the Temple from the surrounding villages. In the second place, even if Jerusalem itself was populous in 458 BC, by 445 it had suffered the sudden disaster which brought Nehemiah from Persia to rebuild the ruins. There is nothing here which calls for a revised chronology.

3. Ezra's thanksgiving for 'a wall in Judah and in Jerusalem' (Ezr. 9:9, RV) has sometimes been taken to refer to Nehemiah's city wall. Few scholars, however, if any, would now appeal to this, since there are various pointers to its being purely a figure of speech. This is indicated by, first, the mention of Judah, which of course had no literal wall round it; secondly by the Hebrew word for 'wall' here (*gāḏēr*, not the *ḥômâ* of Ne. 1:3, *etc.*), which is seldom used for a city wall; thirdly by the fact that in the same breath Ezra has also thanked God for 'a *nail* in his holy place' (9:8)—which no-one takes literally. Rightly therefore RSV translates 'nail' and 'wall' as 'secure hold' and 'protection', and other modern versions make a similar decision.[1]

4. Nehemiah appointed four treasurers over the storehouses (Ne. 13:13), but Ezra, it has been pointed out, found four treasurers already in office when he arrived (Ezr. 8:33)—which might be taken to imply that Nehemiah was the pioneer of this arrangement. As Bright points out, however, this by no means follows, since Nehemiah 'may simply have filled an existing office with honest men'.[2]

5. Some inferences have been drawn from the lists of names associated with the two reformers; but none can be other than tentative, since there are few fathers' names supplied to make identifications certain. Both Ezra and Nehemiah had dealings with men named Meshullam (*e.g.*, Ezr. 8:16; Ne. 3:4), Hashabiah (Ezr. 8:19; Ne. 3:17), Hattush (Ezr. 8:2; Ne. 3:10), Jozabad (Ezr. 8:33; Ne. 11:16), Malchijah (Ezr. 10:31; Ne. 3:11) and Meremoth (Ezr. 8:33; Ne. 3:4, 21). Of these, however, only the last two have fathers' names supplied in both contexts—and Malchijah, of the sons of Harim, could be a

---

[1] NEB, however, retains 'wall' but adds the explanatory words 'of defence'.
[2] J. Bright, *A History of Israel*, p. 394.

member of either of two large clans (*cf.* Ne. 7:35, 42 for these). So Meremoth alone can be positively linked to both Ezra and Nehemiah. From this situation two precarious conclusions have been drawn. The first is that, because none of Ezra's band of homecomers can be *proved* to be identical with their namesakes among Nehemiah's builders, it is therefore safe to maintain that none took part in that exercise; and further, that none may have been in Jerusalem with Nehemiah at all.[1] This, of course, is safe from disproof, but it is not evidence. It is not even an argument from silence; only from ambiguity. And silence itself would have carried less weight here than usual, since in Ezra 8 only thirty-three out of 1,787 homecomers have their names mentioned.

The second inference concerns Meremoth, the one adequately-attested contemporary of both Ezra and Nehemiah. Rowley argues that his double stint of building for Nehemiah (Ne. 3:4, 21) suggests youth and vigour in the year 445, whereas his post as Temple treasurer in Ezra 8:33 points to riper years, conceivably as late as 398 BC, the seventh year of Artaxerxes II. (Rowley, *ibid.*) This is certainly arguable, but is put forward primarily to save the re-dating of Ezra from disproof, and is a little naïve in supposing that the builders in Nehemiah 3 had to be young enough to do a full share of the manual work themselves. The list, which opens with the high priest and which names a number of officials, points rather to the men who were responsible for the various sectors. If anything, the double duty entrusted to Meremoth would imply his maturity rather than his youth.[2]

6. Nehemiah may be thought to have carried out most of his reforms in the somewhat improvised style of a pioneer, and to have been influenced more by Deuteronomy (alleged to be a relatively early product of the law's development) than by the rest of the law. This again might point to his preceding Ezra, especially if Ezra introduced an enlarged law book. One may get this impression of Nehemiah because of his layman's directness, but on closer inspection it emerges that (as W. M. F. Scott[3] and

---

[1] *Cf.* H. H. Rowley, *The Servant of the Lord*, pp. 156ff.; H. L. Ellison, *From Babylon to Bethlehem* (Paternoster, 1976), p. 40.

[2] W. Th. In der Smitten (*Esra*, p. 133, n. 125) argues against Rowley that if Uriah ben Hakkoz was of priestly age at Zerubbabel's return, Rowley's dates would make him improbably old at Meremoth's birth. This, however, assumes more than Ezr. 2:61 says.

[3] W. M. F. Scott, 'Nehemiah–Ezra?', *ET* 58 (1946-7), pp. 263-7.

others have pointed out) four out of his five attacks on abuses, as recorded in the final chapter, were acts implementing the covenant of Nehemiah 10, which arose out of Ezra's 'teach-in'. Brockington makes a similar point, though he is inclined to make Nehemiah rather than Ezra responsible for that covenant's content (*i.e.*, for the details of Ne. 10 : 30–39). But whoever drew it up, that document expresses teachings drawn from the law as a whole, not simply from Deuteronomy.[1] This line of argument, in short, is inconclusive over chronology.

In conclusion, it seems fair to say that none of the major or minor objections to the biblical order of events is compelling, and to point out that nothing stronger than probability is in fact claimed by most scholars for any of the suggested reconstructions. If that is the case, the narrative that we already have must surely take precedence over the narratives that we do not have. And apart from the prior claim of the actual over the hypothetical, nothing that we have discussed is of sufficient weight to counterbalance the vast improbability that our author, devoted as he was to detail, and having access to the first-person records of his principal characters, had no idea of how these men related or failed to relate to one another, nor of who preceded whom. It is an improbability compounded by the necessity to believe that his book, while glaringly at fault over a matter of common knowledge, was accepted as holy writ by a community to which Ezra and Nehemiah were the most recent and among the most honoured of its great men. In contrast to these difficulties, the canonical books in question, studied with due regard to the large area of our ignorance and of their reticence, present no problems to compare with those that beset their alternatives.

### V. EZRA'S BOOK OF THE LAW

Ever since the so-called 'Copernican revolution' in Old Testament criticism, whereby the Mosaic law came to be widely regarded as (at least in its final form) a product of the exile or the subsequent Persian period, interested eyes have been turned towards the book that Ezra brought with him from Babylon.

[1] *Cf.* Brockington, pp. 34, 186, who concludes that 'from this we may infer that the whole Pentateuch was already known in Palestine before it was publicly read by Ezra and accepted by the people in congregation'.

Could this (it was asked) have been the newly-completed Pentateuch?

To reply, with Nehemiah 8:1, that, on the contrary, it was 'the book of the law of Moses which the Lord had given to Israel', is commonly felt to dispose of an interesting question too summarily—not only in view of the widely-held conception of the Pentateuch's slow development through traditions from the south ('J'), the north ('E'), the reform literature known as 'D' (for Deuteronomy) and material from the priestly circles of Jerusalem ('P'), but also in view of the shattering impact which Ezra's reading of it made on his audience, and of some apparent variations between what the Pentateuch prescribes and what Ezra's contemporaries proceeded to do.

U. Kellermann, in the course of expounding his own view of the matter,[1] has listed four main answers given by biblical critics to this question.

1. Ezra's book is seen as *the whole Pentateuch*, in virtually the final stage of its evolution. Within this general view, however, opinions differ as to whether it came as an innovation or not. On the one hand, Rudolph, for example, observes that even if the law struck the hearers as something new (to judge by its profound effect on them) it need not have been new in itself but merely unfamiliar through recent neglect; while Mowinckel from a different angle argues that a great occasion can clothe the most familiar words with new potency, and points out that in matters of religion there is seldom a ready welcome given to innovations.[2] It has also often been remarked that the Samaritans would hardly have accepted the Pentateuch as canonical (while rejecting even the prophets), had it come to them fresh from the hand of Ezra.[3] Again, many have pointed out that Ezra's commission from Artaxerxes takes it for granted that the law in his possession in Babylonia would be recognized in Judah as carrying divine and not only imperial authority; therefore while there may have been differences of practice to resolve between the Babylonian and Palestinian communities, Mowinckel for one sees Ezra's law as a revision of something already widely known as recognized.[4] From another angle, Galling views this public

[1] U. Kellermann, 'Erwägungen zum Esragesetz', *ZAW* 80 (1968), pp. 373-385.
[2] See Rudolph, p. 149; S. Mowinckel, *Studien zu dem Buche Ezra-Nehemia*, III (Oslo, 1965), pp. 129ff.
[3] *Cf.*, *e.g.*, Ackroyd, p. 298; Brockington, p. 23.
[4] Mowinckel, *op. cit.*, esp. pp. 133ff.

ceremony in the context of liturgical proclamations of the law, whose traditional purpose was not to promulgate some new legislation but to actualize (*i.e.*, bring powerfully into the present) what had long existed.[1]

Among those who, on the other hand, reckon that Ezra's Pentateuch imposed a new régime on the hearers, H. Cazelles enlivens the scene by his originality. This writer makes a great point of the provisions in Exodus and Leviticus for equal treatment of the sojourner (*gēr*) and the native (*'ezrāḥ*). He regards this as material specially included to heal the divisions in 5th-century Jewry between the former exiles (whom he sees as the 'sojourners') and those who had remained in the land (the 'natives'). In his view, Nehemiah, preceding Ezra, had so deepened the divisions between the parties of the north and south (both of whom might well appeal to Deuteronomy for vindication, making that book of no use for settling their disputes), that the Persian authorities decided to commission the loyal Jews in Babylon to produce a new codification of religious traditions, to meet this situation. It was with this that Ezra was sent in due course to Jerusalem.

J. G. Vink has hailed this as a brilliant insight; but an eccentricity may be a better word for it—a suspicion confirmed when it emerges that Cazelles and his warmest supporters are not agreed over the intended identity of the very 'sojourners' and 'natives' who form the pivotal point of the hypothesis.[2]

2. A second view is that Ezra's book was the so-called *Priestly Code, i.e.*, the laws in Exodus, Leviticus and Numbers which pentateuchal criticism isolates as handed down or created within the Jerusalem hierarchy. While there is general agreement that ancient material is embedded in it, this collection is usually reckoned by critical scholars to have been edited in Babylonia, either during the exile or in the century that followed it. So it is a tempting speculation that it was Ezra's mission to introduce this material and win acceptance for it. On this view, the completion of the Pentateuch, with its narratives and laws finally edited by this same priestly circle, had not yet taken place in Ezra's day.[3]

---

[1] K. Galling, *Studien zur Geschichte Israels im persischen Zeitalter* (Mohr, 1964), p. 181.

[2] See H. Cazelles, 'La mission d'Esdras', *VT* 4 (1954), pp. 113-140 (esp. pp. 120-122). This article's influence can be seen in P. Grelot, *VT* 6 (1956), pp. 174-189; J. G. Vink, *OTS* 15 (1969), pp. 1-144.

[3] This position finds fewer supporters today than in the earlier days of

3. A more cautious line was taken by, *e.g.*, Kittel, von Rad and Noth, who saw Ezra's law as a compilation of law material which mostly found its way into the Pentateuch, but whose provenance is varied and not always identifiable. Von Rad, for example, points out that in Nehemiah 10 there are some regulations corresponding to 'P' material, some to other sources within the Pentateuch, and some that have no parallel there.[1]

4. Kellermann's fourth group, with which he associates himself with certain reservations, identifies Ezra's document as basically *the law of Deuteronomy*.[2] Kellermann, however, criticizes most of his predecessors in all these groups for their failure to discriminate between admissible and, as he sees it, inadmissible biblical evidence. In his view, the sole source of hard information about Ezra is the letter of Artaxerxes in Ezra 7:12-26, together with possibly the inventory in 8:26f. The rest he pronounces to be *midrash*, *i.e.*, the Chronicler's pious but prejudiced elaboration of this datum and of perhaps some scanty oral tradition. And the last word was left not even to the Chronicler, but to the dissentient voice of a still later editor, the 'Post-Chronistic Redactor'.[3]

From these few approved verses Kellermann argues that Deuteronomy was (basically) Ezra's law book, on the grounds that the law in question was assumed by the king to be already the accepted norm in Judah, and that among the possible candidates for this role the Book of the Covenant had been superseded by Deuteronomy, the so-called Holiness Code (Lv. 17-26) was too specialized and too recently compiled to have acquired such a status, and the so-called Priestly Code, which in his view played no part in the thinking of Malachi or Nehemiah,

---

criticism. Kraus argues tentatively for it (*Worship in Israel* [Blackwell, 1966], pp. 234f., n. 121), and Fohrer does not altogether rule it out (*Introduction to the Old Testament* [Abingdon, 1968], p. 185; but see p. 192).

[1] G. von Rad, *Das Geschichtsbild des chronistischen Werkes*, BWANT 54 (Stuttgart, 1930), pp. 40ff.

[2] *Cf.* R. A. Bowman, *Nehemia: Quellen, Überlieferung und Geschichte*, III (1954), p. 734; L. E. Browne, (*Peake*, pp. 376f.). Kellermann includes W. M. F. Scott, *ET* 58 (1946/7), p. 267, but has misunderstood him. In an *a fortiori* argument Scott refers to Browne's view, but his own position is that Ezra introduced a new law (p. 266).

[3] U. Kellermann, *Nehemia: Quellen, Überlieferung und Geschichte, Beihefte zur ZAW* 102 (1967), pp. 68f. See also his article, cited above, in *ZAW* 80 (1968), esp. pp. 379f. Kellermann's attitude to the source material, and his view that Deuteronomy was Ezra's law, is supported substantially by W. Th. In der Smitten, *Esra: Quellen, Überlieferung und Geschichte*, pp. 124-130.

could hardly have been the code of Ezra, who was Malachi's contemporary and Nehemiah's predecessor.[1] To him, 'P' was probably introduced as a counterblast to Nehemiah's influence, at about the time of the Passover Papyrus of Elephantine (419 BC), some forty years after Ezra's mission.

This rejection of all but about fifteen verses of the Ezra narratives has seemed a little excessive to scholars who practise the same techniques with rather less abandon; but it is hardly surprising that a few writers have carried the process a step further still. O. Kaiser regards even Ezra 7:12-26 as unauthentic, and describes the biblical author as the 'inventor' of the story of Ezra.[2] He is by no means the first to do so, since C. C. Torrey was saying this as long ago as 1896 in even stronger terms.[3] With this view, naturally the identity of Ezra's law becomes a meaningless subject of enquiry.

5. At this point, where historical scepticism reaches the end of its road, we can either draw back to one of the intermediate positions that we have noticed, or take the alternative path of accepting the account at its face value. This has the strength of simplicity, for no-one disputes the fact that, as Mowinckel puts it, 'the author himself did not doubt for a moment that the law book in question, "the law of Moses, which was Yahweh's command to Israel", was the familiar law book which, to him and his contemporaries, had existed and been known ever since the days of Moses.'[4]

Within the books of Ezra and Nehemiah themselves there are no serious obstacles to accepting this view of the matter, for the few difficulties that have been cited are more apparent than real. One such objection is that Nehemiah 8 is surprisingly silent over the Day of Atonement, which was due on the tenth day of the seventh month, followed by Tabernacles on the fifteenth (Lv. 23:27, 34). But our lack of information about events between the second and the fifteenth on this occasion does not entitle us to assume that nothing happened on the tenth, and then to treat this assumption as evidence that the festal dates in Leviticus 23 were not yet known![5] See, further, the commentary on Nehemiah 8:16f.

---

[1] Kellermann argues at length for Ezra's temporal priority over Nehemiah, in *ZAW* 80 (1968), pp. 55-87.

[2] O. Kaiser, *Introduction to the Old Testament* (Eng. tr., Blackwell, 1970), p. 181.

[3] C. C. Torrey, *The Composition and Historical Value of Ezra-Nehemiah* (Giessen, 1896), esp. pp. 58ff.

[4] Mowinckel, *op. cit.*, p. 133; *cf.* p. 136.

[5] L. E. Browne (*Peake*, p. 377a) gratuitously surmises that because the

Another alleged inconsistency with the law is the poll-tax of one-third of a shekel (Ne. 10:32) instead of the half-shekel prescribed in Exodus 30:11-16. This problem, too, is illusory, since the half-shekel was a ransom, levied only when a census was taken, whereas the smaller amount pledged in Nehemiah 10 was an annual payment. The fact that this tax was later raised to the figure that we find in Exodus (Mt. 17:24) cannot be used to make the Exodus law later than Nehemiah, for the Temple tax remained an annual charge, unrelated to the ransom except in its amount and in its use for the expenses of worship.

As we noticed at the outset, a more general objection to the antiquity of Ezra's law is sometimes drawn from the eagerness of the congregation to hear it, and from its powerful effect on them, as of something fresh and new. We have already seen some answers to this (p. 159), and I have also suggested elsewhere (p. 26) that we need look no further than the surrounding scriptures for the ingredients of this explosion of concern—with Malachi's picture of a spiritually starved and disappointed generation, followed by Ezra's sharp thrust to its conscience over the divorce question, and more recently by the sequence of disaster and sudden resurgence described in Nehemiah 1-6. But however excellent these factors may have been as preparations for the word of God, the decisive element was, I suggest, not this kindling material but the fire from heaven—for one can hardly account for the conviction of sin, the rejoicing, the long sessions in Nehemiah 8-10 of instruction, confession and praise, crowned by the act of commitment, except in terms of a movement of the Spirit. These are the marks of what we now call awakenings or revivals. In such cases it is seldom the novelty of what is said or done which is prominent or even present, but rather the opposite: the sudden impact of old truths on newly receptive listeners.

It may still be objected that whatever these people believed about it, modern research has shown that the Pentateuch was not (except in germ) the word of the Lord to Moses but the deposit of a long and chequered history, which had only reached

---

instructions for the Feast of Tabernacles were discovered on the 2nd day of the month (Ne. 8:13f.), the feast itself was held on that day—despite the interval implied in Ne. 8:15 for the widespread proclamation and the preparations, and despite the implication of Ne. 9:1 that by the 24th of the month the eight-day feast at Jerusalem had only recently ended.

the form it now displayed within the lifetime of this congregation or of its recent predecessors. This widely-accepted opinion, however, is the end-product of a naturalistic approach which in my view cannot fail to distort the Pentateuch (or any other scripture), since it conscientiously rules out of its initial reckoning the one thing that sets these writings apart from all others: the direct and all-pervading activity of God in the making of them. This factor is not incidental but integral; therefore to leave it even temporarily out of account is not, as it were, to peel off some outer layer in order to get at the Pentateuch's underlying structure. It is to tear the whole fabric apart, with no possibility of putting it together again un-damaged, as pentateuchal criticism has amply demonstrated. For if (to take a basic example) the laws of the central book of the Pentateuch are indeed what 'the Lord said to Moses'—as almost every chapter of Leviticus takes pains to reiterate—and if they were spoken moreover at mount Sinai nearly forty years before the speeches of Deuteronomy (Lv. 27 : 34; Dt. 1 : 3), then the conclusions of modern criticism (in which Deuteronomy has to precede much of Exodus and Numbers and all of Leviticus, and in which the Lord, if He spoke the gist of these laws, spoke them not to Moses but to his remote successors) offer us not a recovery of the original work but a travesty of it. Such a revised Pentateuch is not merely blemished: it is in almost total disarray.

If this is so, as I believe it to be, a large part of the current debate on Ezra's law book is beside the point. One may legitimately, if inconclusively, discuss how much or little of the Pentateuch Ezra may have read on these occasions,[1] but not how much of it was as yet in being or was the latest thing from Babylon. What the congregation asked for was 'the book of the law of Moses which the Lord had given to Israel'. It was a good request. It deserved and, one need not doubt, received an honest answer.

### VI. EZRA-NEHEMIAH AS HISTORY

While many scholars of all persuasions treat the basic lists,

---

[1] For what it is worth, we can note references in the ensuing chapters, Ne. 9–13, to all five books of Moses: *i.e.*, to the narratives of Gn., Ex., Nu., Dt., in Ne. 9 : 6–22, and to legal material in, *e.g.*, Ex. 13 : 2 (first-born and firstlings, Ne. 10 : 36); in Lv. 23 : 40 (branches for the Feast of Tabernacles, Ne. 8 : 15); in Nu. 18 : 26 (tithe of the tithe, Ne. 10 : 38); in Dt. 23 : 3–5 (Ammonites and Moabites, Ne. 13 : 1f.)—to take a single example from each of Ex., Lv., Nu. and Dt.

letters, edicts and memoirs of these two books as drawn from genuine documents, and the biblical author's use of them as sober and truthful, a number of their predecessors and colleagues have regarded the former as unreliable and the latter as tendentious.

To look first at the period of return and Temple building, we may note that R. Mosis is one who (somewhat exceptionally) dismisses the edict of Cyrus in Ezra 1:2-4 as spurious, and who regards as artificial the account of a substantial return from exile and a prompt start on re-erecting the altar and Temple at the beginning of that reign.[1] The Chronicler, he alleges, has created a *midrash* (an expository study which is somewhat free) on the edicts of Ezra 6:3-5 and 7:11ff., and has likewise freely combined the return and the rebuilding, adapting to his purpose the dates which he found in Haggai and Zechariah and in the Aramaic document preserved in Ezra 4:6 - 6:18. A similarly sweeping revision of our author's sequence of events is carried out by S. Talmon who, having isolated the literary units of which Ezra-Nehemiah appears to be constructed, sets about (as he puts it) 're-evaluating and re-ordering' them. For example, in the account of the return from exile, he detaches the phrase 'the second year' (3:8) from its context, where it indicates a date of *c.* 537 BC, to identify it instead with 'the second year of Darius' nearly a generation later (Ezr. 4:24; Hg. 1:1; Zc. 1:1), *i.e.*, the year 520 BC, with devastating effects on the narrative as we have it. With equal confidence he transfers Ezra 6:19-22a to follow 10:44, thereby obtaining (or, in his view, restoring) a neat sequence of day-and-month dates from the ninth month of one year (Ezr. 10:9) to the first day of the next year (10:17), and on to the Passover held a fortnight later (6:19). This smooth progression, however, conceals considerable feats of agility. It leaps back and forth over a gap of 58 years, and then has to convince us that the 'joy' which irradiated this Passover (6:22) arose not from the dedication of the Temple (6:16ff.) but from Ezra's dissolution of a hundred marriages (10:16-44). These are only two of the rearrangements proposed,[2] but they may serve as samples and as means of comparing the *prima facie* credibility of the existing account with that of some of its alternatives.

[1] R. Mosis, *Untersuchungen zur Theologie des chronistischen Geschichtwerkes* (Herder, 1973), pp. 209ff., 220f.

[2] See S. Talmon, art. 'Ezra and Nehemiah', *IDB Supplementary Vol.* (1976), esp. pp. 321ff.

Coming to the missions of Ezra and Nehemiah (Ezr. 7 - Ne. 13), we meet at once the vexed question whether the canonical account has put the two reformers in the right or the wrong order. This has important implications about the biblical author as historian. Was he accurate or confused? And if he knew the facts, did he respect them or force them to say what he wanted? The chronological question is discussed at some length on pp. 146ff. But speculation has gone far beyond this limited field, in at least three directions, in search of, first, the biblical author's view of the two reformers; secondly, the nature and value of Ezra's and Nehemiah's memoirs; and thirdly, the author's overall outlook and purpose.

1. *The two reformers.* The scepticism of C. C. Torrey and, more recently, O. Kaiser over the very existence of Ezra (see above, p. 162) is a rarity, but a number of scholars distrust the portrait which the Bible gives of him. To W. Th. In der Smitten, for instance, what we are shown in Scripture is chiefly the somewhat idealized Ezra admired increasingly by later generations. So the Chronicler[1] has reinterpreted his status from that of an official, or civil servant, to that of a biblical scholar, by adding to the title 'scribe' the phrase, 'skilled in the law of Moses' (Ezr. 7:6). Perhaps, too, he brings him to Jerusalem twelve years before Nehemiah in order to give him the prestige of a pioneer. Pursuing this fancy, In der Smitten sees the timing of Ezra's reading of the law (and this by popular demand), which takes place just after Nehemiah's personal triumph, as simply another literary artifice of the Chronicler's. How better, he asks, could one put Nehemiah in the shade than by interrupting his memoirs with a block of material (Ne. 8-10) which gives Ezra the limelight? Nehemiah is reduced, he considers, by this means to a mere builder and organizer, whose role was to get things ready for the spiritual giant who was his 'antipodean opposite'.[2]

In this, In der Smitten largely follows the lead of Kellermann, who considered that the Chronicler had strong reasons for deflating the figure of Nehemiah and reducing his work to a mere shadow of Ezra's by this kind of scene-shifting. Not only must Nehemiah's physical achievements be outshone by Ezra's

---

[1] Most writers on these books mean by this term the author of the books of Chronicles, whom they regard as also the author of Ezra and Nehemiah. Where I use the term for the author of these two latter books, I intend it only as a synonym for 'historian' or 'author', for reasons given on pp. 136f.

[2] W. Th. In der Smitten, *Esra: Quellen, Überlieferung und Geschichte,* esp. pp. 65f.

spiritual ones, but even his religious reforms must be transferred to a postscript (Ne. 13), so as to appear to be no more than implementing the 'firm covenant' of chapter 10, the work of Ezra.[1] If we protest that in fact the text does not support this charge of biased history writing (since Ne. 8:9 shows Nehemiah playing an active part at the reading of the law, and Ne. 10:1 shows him heading the list of signatories to the 'firm covenant'), a number of modern voices will reply that these mentions of Nehemiah are doubtless the insertions of a subsequent redactor who is determined to correct his predecessor's version of events. This hypothetical redactor is then furnished, by some, with a date in the Maccabean era, about 150 BC.[2]

The motives for these postulated moves and counter-moves will be discussed in the final section (3, below). Meanwhile we may notice some opinions on what are ostensibly two first-hand sources for the historian: the first-person accounts found in Ezra and Nehemiah.

2. *The Ezra memoirs and Nehemiah memoirs.* These passages written in the first person are listed on pp. 134f., and there is a brief discussion on pp. 136ff. of their relation to the book as a whole.

Critical opinion, which readily accepts Nehemiah's memoirs as authentic, is hesitant or dismissive over Ezra's, some scholars treating them as pure invention modelled by the Chronicler on those of Nehemiah, while others allow them to be ultimately derived from Ezra but considerably modified in the editing. Even Nehemiah, however, while accepted as the writer of his own record, has not escaped suspicion of improving on the facts, for Kellermann feels it necessary to make use of '*Tendenz*-criticism'— that is, to identify the impression the writer is wanting to create, and make appropriate allowance for it, reckoning that he would at least suppress whatever was unfavourable to his case, even if he told no lies. Kellermann in fact conjectures that in one instance if no other (Ne. 6:10ff.) Nehemiah went further than suppression, to cover up a politically embarrassing incident with a set of falsehoods.[3] We are left with a choice between taking Nehemiah's word for what happened and Kellermann's for what might have happened,

---

[1] U. Kellermann, *Nehemia: Quellen, Überlieferung und Geschichte, Beihefte zur ZAW* 102 (1967), pp. 69, 90–92.
[2] See, *e.g.*, S. Mowinckel, *Studien, I*, pp. 45ff.; U. Kellermann, *op. cit.*, p. 105; J. G. Vink, *OTS* 15 (1969), pp. 28–30.
[3] U. Kellermann, *Nehemia*, pp. 88, 179ff. See also below, p. 999, on Shemaiah.

and with a general warning from the latter against too readily taking Nehemiah's side in his exchanges with his opponents.

This raises the question of Nehemiah's motive in putting these things on record. Are they simply memoirs, or something more? To this a number of answers have been offered.

More than one writer has seen a likeness between Nehemiah's narrative and various memorial inscriptions of ancient times, whether royal, votive or funerary. Mowinckel[1] was reminded of the monuments of early near-eastern kings, and reckoned that the substance of Nehemiah's account was not too long to be inscribed on a stele little larger than the well-known Moabite Stone of King Mesha.[2] He suggested that God's promise to eunuchs of a memorial in His house (Is. 56:4f.) inspired Nehemiah to compose this piece for erection in the Temple. This is an ingenious conjecture, but even apart from the lack of proof that Nehemiah was a eunuch (see on Ne. 1:11) or desired a public monument, there is a glaring contrast between these boastful inscriptions and his sober, workmanlike report.

Nearer the mark, one may feel, is von Rad's comparison of these memoirs with some tomb and temple inscriptions of Egyptian priests and officials of roughly Nehemiah's time and rank, recounting their faithful execution of their duties, their altruism (not unlike Nehemiah's in Ne. 5:14ff.) and in some cases their measures to rectify religious abuses (*cf.* Ne. 13).[3] Since the object of such Egyptian memorials was recognition by God and also man, some of them address the reader directly, as well as offering a prayer for divine remembrance—whereas Nehemiah only does the latter. While von Rad, if I understand him, does not see Nehemiah's composition as an intended memorial tablet, but rather as a scroll to be deposited in the Temple (*cf.*, he suggests, Ps. 40:7), he seems to overstate his case in some of the alleged signs of Egyptian influence which he adduces (*e.g.*, the expression, 'my God had put into my heart . . .', 2:12; *cf.* 7:5; and even—although tentatively—Nehemiah's account of the pressure that was on him by day and night). But he does recognize the distinctiveness of the biblical material, especially in Nehemiah's emphasis on personal guidance, his prayerfulness,

---

[1] S. Mowinckel, *Studien*, II, *e.g.*, pp. 81f.

[2] He admits, however, that with nearly seven times the number of letters to fit in, the writing would have to be smaller and more compact, and the pillar four-sided.

[3] *ZAW* 76 (1964), pp. 176-187.

and his robust confidence that God will not fail His servants. The vividness of detail, the candour, the preoccupation with God rather than with the reader, stand out in refreshing contrast to the more generalized and sententious self-portraits of the Egyptians.

Instead, however, of writing with an eye to posterity, could it be that Nehemiah was composing his defence against slanders that were threatening his position? Kellermann, noting some varieties of this view of the document (as an apologia for presentation to Artaxerxes, or as an example of the prayers of those who are falsely accused, as found in the psalter) sees it as a combination of manward apologia and Godward appeal for vindication, in a context where false witnesses were certain to discredit his version of events, and where priests would not assist him to present his prayer at the Temple. He must therefore look to God's unmediated 'remembrance', *i.e.*, intervention on his behalf.[1]

While a reasonable case can be made out for some of these views, it is important to remember that the evidence for any one of them is very slender: a resemblance here or there to other writings, or an indication of party strife and therefore of rumours that would call for a reply. We shall look at the latter point in the next section, but meanwhile it is worth reflecting that the most obvious hypothesis may well be the strongest—namely that Nehemiah wrote these things as spontaneously as he did everything else. That his memoirs (to use this convenient term) have a flavour all their own is almost the only point on which all scholars seem agreed; and we may add to this the fact that Nehemiah was one of the best organized and most godly administrators to be found in Scripture. As such, it would seem to be well in character that he should keep a record of what he did, and that he should do so in the form of a report to his divine Master. Some of his material seems to have been written in the thick of events (see the comment on Ne. 4:4, 5); and the man who darted a prayer to God between hearing the king's question and replying to it (2:4) is recognizably the man whose prayer, 'Remember me!', punctuates and signs off his written account of the mission he fulfilled.

3. *The historian's purpose.* Probably most readers, and certainly the present writer, would reckon that to record the rebuilding of

---

[1] U. Kellermann, *Nehemia*, pp. 76ff., esp. p. 85.

Israel's life and institutions in the first century after the exile, in the midst of a gentile world which was part enemy, part protector and governor, part seducer, and to show God's providence in raising up the leaders who would hold her to her vocation as a people apart, centred on God's Temple and city and law, was the principal aim and achievement of the biblical author. But some scholars read almost more between the lines than in the narrative itself, to arrive at a radical reappraisal first of the scenes presented and then of the character and fundamental purpose of this pair of books.

In a number of studies it has become a central preoccupation to discover here the traces of continuing party conflicts in pre-Christian Judaism, both in germ, *i.e.*, in the events which are the subject-matter of Ezra–Nehemiah, and, more fully, in the editor's presentation of them. This can be illuminating but it can also be overdone. One begins to see everything in terms of a conflict between the eschatological aspirations of one party which could be loosely called Messianic or Zionist (fed, it is suggested, by the glowing prophecies of such passages as Is. 60–62), and the more static outlook of the priestly element and of the well-to-do, who saw no reason to look too earnestly for a new age or to keep aloof from their influential neighbours. Certainly one cannot read these narratives without encountering some such tension between the worldly and the uncompromising; but there is enough spelt out in the record without forcing it to yield still more.

For instance (to take an example first put forward by Sellin in 1898, and taken up at intervals by others) it outruns the evidence to picture Zerubbabel as a hothead who tried to set up as the Davidic king, only to be suppressed and therefore disappear from the narrative after Ezra 5:2. Likewise it is tempting to construct from such a prophecy as Jeremiah 33:14–26 a story of Messianic hopes that had failed with Zerubbabel but were fanned into flame again with the coming of Nehemiah;[1] but

---

[1] The prophecy is a promise of a never-failing throne of David and a never-failing levitical priesthood. On the assumption that such an oracle will have grown out of a situation that calls for it, one can build up an imagined setting of disappointed expectations and a need of reassurance over the Messiah and/or the priesthood; and finally one can seek a historical situation to match these features. The prophecy is dated accordingly, and ascribed if necessary to a prophet other than the one who is its traditional author. In this case, the critical consensus places it in the post-exilic age. It will be seen, I think, that every link in this chain is an assumption, however safe one may judge any one of them to be.

again there is a shortage of supporting facts. Kellermann, however, is confident that one can trace the existence of a Messianic party in Jerusalem not only in the days of Zerubbabel (whose eclipse is thought by H. Gese to have extinguished the expectation of the coming Prince (*nāśī'*) of Ezekiel 44:1-3, *etc.*)[1] but as a potent force in the days of Nehemiah. In this reading of events, while Nehemiah is not thought to have encouraged the hopes pinned to him, he is conceived to have been a Davidide—for Kellermann sees his allusion to the city of his 'fathers' sepulchres' as a hint of royal descent (Ne. 2:5; *cf.* Ezk. 43:7 f.), borne out later by Sanballat's accusation of a bid for the throne (Ne. 6:6f.) and by Nehemiah's initiative in proclaiming a release of debts (like King Zedekiah's initiative over slaves in Je. 34:8ff.; *cf.* Ne. 5:6ff.). These are only wisps of evidence, but on this basis Kellermann radically rewrites the story of Shemaiah's attempt to lure Nehemiah into the Temple (6:10ff.). This now becomes a plot to have him crowned in secret; and although the plot fails through Nehemiah's refusal, it helps to discredit him. So his return to Babylon after twelve years (Ne. 5:14; 13:6) is interpreted, on this theory, as his recall to answer charges of disloyalty or of failure to govern peaceably. Further, his so-called memoirs are understood as the defence he has prepared, and his interjected appeals to God indicate that he can count on little human support when he comes to trial. As for his second spell as governor (Ne. 13), which would seem to contradict this version of what happened, Kellermann dismisses it as an editorial invention. Chapter 13, he considers, should be modified and placed near the beginning of the book, to describe what awaited Nehemiah when he first arrived at Jerusalem.

As if this were not enough re-reading of the data, Kellermann distinguishes, as we have seen above (p. 167), two rival editorial estimates of Nehemiah. One was by a second-century redactor who saw him as a successor of Zerubbabel and a forerunner of the Hasmonean priest-kings—the priest-like founder of the post-exilic cult-community and the king-like founder of the post-exilic state. The other estimate was that of the Chronicler, who arranged his materials so as to have him overshadowed at every point by Ezra, reducing him to little more than a building contractor for the Persians.[2]

[1] H. Gese, *Der Verfassungsentwurf des Ezechiel*, Beiträge zur historischen Theologie, 25 (1957), p. 119.
[2] U. Kellermann, *Nehemia*, esp. pp. 89-111; 174-204.

We have already touched on some division of opinion over Ezra and his mission (pp. 146-158), giving only a small sample of a large debate; but the concern of the present section is not so much with the characters and events in themselves as with the way they are handled in the biblical account. What are the views and aims which have supposedly shaped these books? To what extent are we dealing with actual events and sequences, and with true interpretation; and to what extent, if any, with a picture touched up and re-touched in the interests of rival factions?

Some of the most influential voices—though indeed not all—would reply at once that much of what passes here for history is not a record but a retrojection: that is, a description of the present in the guise of the past, to give current practices the prestige of antiquity and of association with great names; and further, that one must discern here not only the partisan approach of a single historian but (as we have seen) the dissent of a subsequent corrector, from another age and party.[1]

The favourite example of both these suggested phenomena—retrojection and rival histories—is the account of Ezra's reading of the law in Nehemiah 8, which has already occupied us in another connection (see above, pp. 158-164). Since some of the procedures of that great day are also found in synagogue worship (such as the benediction before the reading, the standing of the congregation, the exposition of the law), it can be argued that the Chronicler was only reading back his own customs into a former and more illustrious age. He is also suspected, as already mentioned, of scoring party points by rudely interrupting the approaching climax of Nehemiah's memoirs, by inserting this block of material that ignores him in favour of Ezra (Ne. 8-10)—material which should have rounded off Ezra 8 or Ezra 10.

If we point out that Nehemiah is not in fact ignored here, but is present and prominent (Ne. 8:9; 10:1), it will either be replied that these statements are copying errors (twice) or that they are the work of the pro-Hasmonean redactor mentioned above (p. 167), as a corrective to the Chronicler's bias. They are not evidence of what happened (we are assured), any more than is the rival version.

Indeed, scepticism is at times so extreme as to collapse into an

---

[1] Cf., among many, R. Mosis, op. cit., pp. 14, 229; K.-F. Pohlmann, Studien zum dritten Esra (Göttingen, 1970), pp. 136, 151ff.; W. Th. In der Smitten, op. cit., p. 67; U. Kellermann, op. cit., p. 29; J. G. Vink, OTS 15 (1969), p. 33.

implausibility of which it seems somewhat anxiously aware. We are warned by one writer, for example, against being captivated by the vividness of Ezra 3:13 (the mingled shout of joy and lamentation), and are instructed to read this purely as the Chronicler's device to emphasize the second Temple's limitations. It must not be factual.[1] Another writer is embarrassed by the credibility of the 'heavy rain' which cut short the proceedings in Ezra 10:13. This 'picturesque detail about the rainfall' is only allowed to remind us 'of apocryphal literature', and to contribute to the conclusion that 'the two chapters concerning Ezra's measures in the matter of mixed marriages are unauthentic and legendary', throwing light only on 'the Jewish minority so hard-pressed in the Maccabean period'.[2]

Between this degree of disbelief and the comparative conservatism of some recent commentaries there is a wide difference; nevertheless on the basic conviction that the Chronicler (so-called) has embroidered and re-shaped the past in the colours and contours of his own age there is little disagreement among critical scholars. What appears to be history is thus held to be partisan theology or ecclesiology, bending the past to the service of the present or, more accurately, to the service of the hieratic party against the zealots, and (with the redactor) back again in the interests of the latter.

But it is of utmost importance to realize that this low estimate of Ezra–Nehemiah's factual content is not ultimately based on intrinsic improbabilities of the story told there. This or that detail may strike one scholar as probable, another as improbable; but perfectly good sense can be made of the whole sequence, including the much-attacked Nehemiah 8–10 in the position in which we find it. The roots of this scepticism lie elsewhere and much deeper, namely in pentateuchal criticism as generally practised. One must finally, at the risk of being tedious, come back to this.

If one takes the view that the full code of so-called priestly laws of the Pentateuch and the elaborate choirs and guilds that staffed the Temple were the product not of Moses and David but of the post-exilic age, then one has to treat the books of Chronicles, Ezra and Nehemiah (whether they are of common authorship or not) as drastically-doctored history. There is no alternative, for we are presented in these books with these institutions

R. Mosis, *op. cit.*, p. 221.
[2] J. G. Vink, *OTS* 15 (1969), p. 33

apparently known in full many centuries before the exile, and rebuilt on professedly the old foundations as soon as possible after it. Chronicles devotes many chapters to David's founding of the guilds, and gives us, as do Ezra and Nehemiah, an abundance of names and of extracts from duty rotas to provide no mere sketch of an imagined or ideal community, but what purports to be a slice of life within the Temple courts and the levitical traditions, at points in history when most schemes of pentateuchal criticism allow them no such existence. The book of Ezra presents us almost at the outset with a register in which priests and Levites, so far from being still undifferentiated, appear as long-established and distinct orders, conscious of their separate pedigrees; while certain families among the Levites are by long tradition either singers or gatekeepers; after which the story that unfolds shows them functioning not by an evolving liturgy but 'as it is written in the law of Moses' and 'according to the directions of David king of Israel' (Ezr. 3:2, 10).

Faced with this evidence, one can either accept its confirmation of the Pentateuch's antiquity, or else conclude, with the majority of the scholars whom we have sampled, that Chronicles, Ezra and Nehemiah (and the Pentateuch itself) are what the New Testament would bluntly call 'cunningly devised fables' (2 Pet. 1:16, AV). One should resist the temptation, I suggest, to put the matter more gently. There is no merit in putting up memorials to the prophets we dismember. If, however, (as I believe) these books are 'true, and righteous altogether', then their record of God's laws and ways, and of His providence in seeing His purpose through to fulfilment, can speak as strongly to us as to the first participants in these seminal events.